Book of Love Poetry

The Wordsworth

Book of Love Poetry

Selected, with an Introduction,
by Ella Masson

Wordsworth Poetry Library

This edition published 1995 by Wordsworth Editions Ltd,
Cumberland House, Crib Street, Ware, Hertfordshire SG12 9ET.

The publishers gratefully acknowledge permission to include
poems by Ursula Vaughan Williams and Kathleen Raine.

Reprinted 1996

ISBN 1-85326-445-8

Printed and bound in Great Britain
by Mackays of Chatham plc, Chatham, Kent

INTRODUCTION

The poems in this anthology have been selected exclusively from work composed in the English language. No translations have been included, although some of the sixteenth and, particularly, seventeenth-century verse may echo the classical originals that inspired them. The thematic arrangement arose after the poetry had been collected, and is thus largely dictated by the preoccupations of poets across the ages rather than by a structure into which their work was required to fit.

The spelling adopted for some poems, notably those published before the mid-nineteenth century, does not necessarily reflect the style in which they were originally presented. For ease of reading, capitalisation and italicisation have, in the main, been replaced by standard lower case roman text. Similarly, some of the more distracting uses of apostrophes have been removed, except where they bear on the scansion of a line. Thus, 'best resolv'd' is rendered as 'best resolved', but 'thou gett'st not me' stays as it is. Stress marks (rendered as a French grave accent) have been included where a modern reader might easily miss a syllable that is now commonly contracted but which was originally intended to be pronounced.

The birthday of my life is come, my love is come to me

The sheer exuberance and lightness of heart that falling in love can provoke and the sensation of life being utterly transformed are feelings well expressed by many of the poets in the first section of the book. A little-known American poet, May Thielgaard Watts, reports, 'To-day there have been lovely things/I never saw before,' and concludes by way of explanation, 'My love kissed my eyes last night.' Rupert Brooke, in 'The Great Lover' develops the idea of how the illuminating experience of love can promote a charmed engagement with life in general. Here too are gentle, affectionate, heartfelt declarations of love, often alluding to the natural world, as in the extract from Dante Gabriel Rossetti's poem, 'The House of Life', in which he looks down at his lover lying 'in the long fresh grass' with 'billowing skies' above and 'golden kingcup-fields' all around: 'So this winged hour is dropped to us from above . . . This close-companioned inarticulate hour/When two-fold silence was the song of love.' There are lovers enjoining each other to love truly: 'If thou must love me, let it be for nought/Except for love's sake only' (Barrett Browning) and 'Pray love me little, so you love me long' (Herrick); declarations of constancy – 'Earth, heaven, fire, air, the world transformed shall view,/Ere I prove false to faith, or strange to you! (Dowland) – and musings as to why one ever falls in love with a particular person at all. The mysterious 'Ephelia', a 17th-century poet whose true identity remains obscure, retorts: 'Go, ask the glorious sun, why every day it round the world doth run', and her near contemporary Alexander Brome admits, 'I/Do know I love, but know not how, nor why.' John Clare and Caroline Norton, both writing in the first half of the nineteenth century, declare confidently: 'I do not love thee', and then go on to evoke the maddeningly contradictory feelings falling in love can provoke. A few find it difficult to put their emotions into words: 'My passion would lose by expression', explains Lady Mary Wortley Montagu, and Elizabeth Barrett Browning refers to the 'love hid in me out of reach'.

What thing is love?
'Love' declared the seventeenth-century Sidney Godolphin, 'Is ever a mixed sense/Of what we have, and what we want' and for all the numerous attempts that have been made to define it, his words perhaps best explain the perplexity which descends on those who try to define this most pervasive, yet elusive experience. Sometimes, the poet is unequivocal: Mallet refers to a 'soft divinity', Wilmot to 'the most generous passion of the mind', and Drayton pronounces 'life is my love/love is my whole felicity.' But often there is a keen sense of the contradictory nature of this emotion: Aphra Behn's 'pleasing delusion, witchery divine', Shakespeare's 'choking gall, and a preserving sweet' and Lyly's 'a heat full of coldness, a sweet full of/Bitterness' all express this ambivalence. Emily Dickinson provides perhaps the most compact – and arcane – definition: 'Love is anterior to life./Posterior to death, Initial of creation, and/The exponent of breath.' There seems no answer to that, except, perhaps, James Hogg's 'O, love, love, love!/Love is like a dizziness;/It winna let a poor body/Gang about his biziness!'

O so white, O so soft, O so sweet is she
The second section brings together a selection from the many poems in the well-worked vein of admiration for a loved one, often expressed in highly idealised terms. Here it is almost exclusively a male voice that is to be heard, speaking of 'matchless whiteness', of lips like cherries and cheeks like roses. Perhaps the most stylised contribution is from Richard Leigh who writes a delicately constructed account of how the

air around his 'charming fair' ('Lady With A Fan') mourns the fact that after 'a snatched embrace' it cannot help but be replaced by 'new winds'. Ben Jonson's 'O so white, O so soft, O so sweet is she!' encapsulates this other-worldly, courtly tradition, an approach neatly debunked by Shakespeare in 'My Mistress' Eyes Are Nothing Like The Sun': 'Coral is far more red than her lip's red:/If snow be white, why then her breasts are dun;/If hairs be wires, black wires grow on her head.' And Mary Leapor supplies a cynical interpretation of the dubious motives lying behind a male admirer's soft words. Some admirers have been entranced by an alluring dress sense: 'Then, then (methinks,) how sweetly flows/That liquefaction of her clothes' savours Herrick, who voices his approval in another poem of 'a sweet disorder in the dress', as does Jonson in his 'robes loosely flowing, hair as free'. Others, though rather alarmingly few, go for more intellectual pleasures, as 'What perfect form can him beguile?/Who doats upon thy perfect mind' (Frank Sayers).

Despair, whose torments no men, sure, but lovers and the damned endure
'For he that sees the heaven he misses/Sustains two hells, of love and pain (Stanley). The miserable experience of unrequited love has proved fertile ground for many poets, and most aspects of this unhappy state (including the dismay of the recipient of unwanted advances) have been explored. 'Hers will I be, and only with this thought/Content myself, although my chance be nought', wails Henry Howard hopelessly, and 'I did but crave that I might kiss, If not her lip, at least her hand/Soon, if my love by you were crowned, Fair prophetess, my grief would cease' (Flatman). Small wonder that Mary Chudleigh is moved to pose and answer the question: Tell me, Marissa, by what rule/May I judge who's the greatest fool?/*Marissa* I'll tell you, since you can't discover!/It is an awkward whining lover'; Mrs Barbauld gently advises a love-lorn admirer to 'Drag no more a hopeless chain'. Some dissatisfied lovers are merely miserable, others turn petulant: 'Nothing in the world is single' remarks Shelley crossly, 'All things by a law divine/In one spirit meet and mingle./Why not I with thou?' And some recover their sense of self-preservation to lay down an ultimatum: 'Give me more love, or more disdain' (Carew); 'If she slight me when I woo/I can scorn and let her go,/For if she be not for me/What care I for whom she be.' (Wither). Still others eventually find solace in dreams: Michael Field (actually an aunt and niece couple writing under this pseudonym) invokes sleep – 'thou child of night' – to 'Give me thy dreams, thy lies./Lead through

the horny portal white/The pleasure day denies.' A few poets express
the sadness of those unable to reciprocate offering of heartfelt affection:
'Am I cold,/Ungrateful,' asks Barrett Browning, 'that for these most
manifold/High gifts, I render nothing back at all?' and Edward
Thomas, deeply subdued, admits, 'For I at most accept/Your love, re-
gretting/That is all: I have kept/Only a fretting/That I could not
return/All that you gave/And could not burn/With the love you have.'

Love's delusive fatal snare

In the traditional war between the sexes, one of the most familiar
scenarios is that of a man attempting to persuade a reluctant woman
to succumb to his advances. The seduction is frequently treated as a
form of battle or hunting involving a pursuit, and – with skill and a
touch of luck – a male victory or conquest. A less than enthusiastic
response on the woman's part simply provokes a greater onslaught of
what would politely be called persuasion, but often sounds more like
bullying, on the simple principle that a female 'no' could be taken as
'yes', if enough pressure was applied. The elusive prey was in the main
considered teasing, duplicitous, coy. People most certainly do, and
always will, play games and lead each other on – teasing and flirting
have never gone out of fashion – but now that some of the rather
plaintive responses of women poets to this 'game' are resurfacing, we
are reminded that the stakes for the female sex were sometimes cata-
strophically high. Such were the double standards of society, that while
a woman was chided for not giving way to the blandishments of a
man, she was also respected only if she kept her honour intact. ('A
treasure thou has lost today! For which thou can'st no ransom pay',
chides Randolph.) Before effective contraception, any breaches of this
code, any giving in to indulgence – either of self or of a partner – could
lead to the ultimately shaming proof of misdoing and social ruin. Only
occasionally do male poets refer to the wretched plight of women
deemed to have lost their honour, though Philip Frowde creates a
powerful image of a woman's 'hapless beauty' having just reached fru-
ition, 'when comes the savage, the despoiler, man/With hand rapacious
ravages the boughs,/And leaves her naked, stripped of all her honours.'

On the whole, though, it is unsurprisingly the female poets who con-
centrate on this theme: 'Soft kisses may be innocent', warns Catherine
Cockburn, 'But ah! too easy maid beware;/Tho' that is all thy kind-
ness meant,/'Tis love's delusive, fatal snare.' 'Ye virgin powers! defend
my heart/From amorous looks and smiles . . . if thro' passion I grow

blind, Let honour be my guide.' says Mrs Taylor, stoutly defending her corner, but realising she is her own worst enemy. The persuaders, on the other hand, have only to concern themselves with how best to snare their prey, and one of the favourite tactics seems to be to warn of the perils of advancing age, the ravages that time will effect on a woman's beauty, and therefore the urgent necessity to make full use of these advantages while there is still time. 'The cruel tyrant that did kill those flow'rs, Shall once (aye me!) not spare that spring of yours (Drummond)'; 'Thou may'st repent that thou has scorned my tears, when winter snows upon thy sable hairs' (Daniel); 'For having lost but once your prime,/You may for ever tarry' (Herrick). These are a few of the endless variations on the theme. Alexander provides an apparent appreciation of a woman remaining aloof, only to deliver a stinging warning: 'But do not fall in love with thine own self/Narcissus erst was lost on such a shelf'. It is, however, Carew who indulges in the most shameless manipulation: Starve not thyself, because you may/Thereby make me pine away.' As this seems to have been a somewhat unequal conquest, I leave the last word to Aphra Behn, 'Oh how I fell like a long-worshipped idol/Discovering all the cheat.'

Fire and fetters

'A heart,' warns Cockburn, 'whose safety but in flight does lie,/Is too far lost to have the power to fly', and Trefusis pronounces, 'When to love's influence woman yields,/She loves for life! and daily feels/Progressive tenderness! – each hour/Confirms, extends the tyrant's power.' 'Remember', contributes Killigrew, 'When you love, from that same hour/Your peace you put into your lover's power.' But the complaint is by no means confined to women. Campion counsels, 'Lost is our freedom When we submit to women so.' So constricting and painful are the fetters of love, that sometimes no love at all can seem preferable; Jan Struther, writing in this century, declares exultantly, 'I have been long a slave, and now am free ... I have been caged, and now I hold the key,' echoing Wyatt's sentiments some four hundred years earlier: 'Farewell, love, and all thy laws for ever:/Thy baited hooks shall tangle me no more.'

My thirsty soul kept watch for one away

The section entitled *Absence* is deliberately restricted to evocations of being without one's lover, rather than examining why this sad state has come about. In his Lucia's absence, says Joseph Addison, 'Life hangs upon me, and becomes a burden', and Anne Bradstreet compares herself to a 'loving hind that (hartless) wants her deer'. Fanny Kemble and

Christina Rossetti contrast the misery of being alone with the ecstasy
of being with their lovers: 'And all I am, or know, or feel is thee;/My
soul grows faint, my veins run liquid flame! (Kemble); 'At length there
came the step upon the stair . . . There first my spirit seemed to scent
the air/Of paradise: then first the tardy sand/Of time ran golden, and
I felt my hair/Put on a glory, and my soul expand' (Rossetti).

Pale hag, infernal fury, pleasure's smart

Shakespeare's 'green-eyed monster' raises its head briefly. Sir William
Davenant's analysis of jealousy is among the most illuminating: ''Tis
love that has lost itself in a mist;/'Tis love being frighted out his wits;/
'Tis love that has a fever got...' Jonson is determined not to capitulate to
this dead-end of an emotion: 'I ne'er will owe my health to a disease.'
William Blake's famous 'He who binds himself to a joy/Does the wingèd
life destroy' is touchingly prefigured by Elijah Fenton's 'I, whose life/
Was bound to thine, by striving to secure/Thy beauties all my own,
have killed the dove/I fondly grasped too close.'

Such falso soft sighs

In *Treachery & Deceit*, full vent is given to the bitterness of love betrayed.
Men accuse women of deceit and inconstancy, and women accuse men
of inconstancy and deceit. 'Oh, my hard fate!' says Nathaniel Lee, 'Why
did I trust her ever?' What story is not full of woman's falsehood?/The
sex is all a sea of wide destruction'. 'Men are unconstant, and delight
to range' complains 'Ephelia', 'Not to gain freedom, but their fetters
change:/And what a year ago they did with passion seek,/Grows
troublesome, and nauseous in a week.' Vituperation abounds, and the
wounded party invariably claims the moral high ground. Thomas's
'Forsaken Wife' concludes a tirade against her unfaithful husband with
'I yet superior am to you', and Sir Robert Ayton spitefully remarks, 'And
I shall sigh, when some will smile,/To see thy love to every one/Hath
brought thee to be loved by none.'

A moment's heaven pays back an age of hell

Almost every poet who has even toyed with the subject of love has
been unable to resist the temptation to expound (sometimes at great
length) upon its pains. Blake's garden of love turns out to be 'filled with
graves ... And priests in black gowns ... binding with briars my joys
and desires'. Frances Greville's most famous poem 'A Prayer For
Indifference' accepts wearily, 'I ask no kind return of love . . . 'Tis bliss
but to a certain bound,/Beyond is agony.' Regrets over love that does

not materialise, or complaints that its path fails to run smooth, are legion. 'My name is Might-have been;' writes Dante Gabriel Rossetti, 'I am also called No-more, Too-late, Farewell'. Helen Hunt Jackson and D.H. Lawrence, writing respectively at the end of the nineteenth and beginning of the twentieth century, deal with two aspects of conflict and disappointment that may seem alarmingly familiar: a wife bemoaning her husband's failure to remember an important anniversary; a man, whose partner has clearly requested some insight into his emotions, angrily denying that he has any such feelings. Mathilde Blind reveals her bruises in her pathetic inquiry: 'Did you win, or did I lose?'

My true-love hath my heart, and I have his
In spite of all the 'fever and the fret', there is plenty of evidence of the thrill and deep satisfaction that mutual affection can deliver. Wives prize husbands, 'If ever two were one, then surely we./If ever man were loved by wife, then thee' (Bradstreet), and husbands value wives: 'Teacher, tender, comrade, wife, A fellow farer true through life' (Stevenson) and 'There is no happy life but in a wife' (Cavendish). There is, however, no shortage of poets, notably female (among them Mary Barber, Susanna Blamire, Mary Savage and Lady Mary Wortley Montagu), offering advice on marriage and warning of the disadvantages (to put it mildly) of the conjugal state. Mehetabel Wright rails against 'this source of discord, pain and care/Thou sure forerunner of despair.' Jane Barker is not at all sure that she needs the aggravation of marriage, and Sarah Egerton politely eschews it completely: 'Nor do I think there's a necessity/For all to enter beds, like Noah's beasts/Into his ark.'

Weep eyes, break heart . . . my love and I must part
The near-universal experience of parting is another predictably well-covered subject. A tiny extract from one of Dryden's plays expresses the almost physical pain of a couple being torn apart: 'Heav'n knows how loth I am to part from thee:/So from the seal is softened wax disjoined:/ So from the mother plant the under rind.' And Amy Lowell contributes a modern lament: 'When I go away from you/The world beats dead/Like a slackened drum.' There are words of anger when parting is necessitated by the breakdown of a relationship: 'Give, give me back that trifle you despise/Give back my heart, with all its injuries' (Dixon), and sorrowful regrets, 'Words are so weak/When love hath been so strong (Dowson). And the famous and bruisingly matter-of-fact advice from Drayton: 'Since there's no help, come let us kiss and part,/Nay I have done; you get no more of me.'

The pillar perished is whereto I leant

The saddest and most poignant poems mourn the loss of a loved one. In spite of its extreme brevity, Martha Brewster's 'Oh! – he – is – gone' never fails to touch me. Similarly, 'He first deceased: she for a little tried/ To live without him: liked it not, and died' (Wotton) is affecting in its simplicity. Among all the mourning and the agony is Henry King's interesting and rather upbeat 'Legacy', in which he encourages his future widow to find a new partner to 'supply my room when I am gone': 'I would not have/Thy youth and beauty married to my grave'. He even provides her with a rationale: ''Twould show thou didst repent the style of wife/Should'st thou relapse into a single life.' He concludes generously: 'So will the stock of our affection thrive/No less in death, than were I still alive./And in my urn I shall rejoice, that I/Am both Testatour thus and legacy.'

The introductions to virtually all anthologies of love poetry contain a whiff of apology, a sense that the compiler was rather happier to riffle through the quantities of verse written on the subject (and to indulge personal preferences and prejudices) than to explain or justify the resulting selection. The richness of English love poetry is such that almost any selection will elicit regret that a favourite has been missed out, or incomprehension as to why certain poems have found their way in. The compiler can only hope that there are enough pleasant surprises and glows of recognition to offset disappointments of this nature. Love poetry, perhaps more than any other thematic selection, is likely to be highly individual and personal in its appeal. Whether or not the poems strike a chord may have as much to do with personal experience, hopes or fears, as with the literary quality of the work. In spite of all this, I hope the selection will be as enjoyable in the reading as it was in the compiling.

CONTENTS

SONGS OF LOVE

A Birthday

My heart is like a singing bird
    Whose nest is in a watered shoot;
My heart is like an apple-tree
    Whose boughs are bent with thick-set fruits;
My heart is like a rainbow shell
    That paddles in a halcyon sea;
My heart is gladder than all these,
    Because my love is come to me.

Raise me a daïs of silk and down;
    Hang it with vair and purple dyes;
Carve it in doves and pomegranates,
    And peacocks with a hundred eyes;
Work it in gold and silver grapes,
    In leaves and silver fleurs-de-lys;
Because the birthday of my life
    Is come, my love is come to me.

CHRISTINA ROSSETTI

When I Heard At The Close Of The Day

When I heard at the close of the day how my name had
    been receiv'd with plaudits in the capitol, still it
    was not a happy night for me that follow'd,
And else when I carous'd, or when my plans were accomplish'd,
    still I was not happy,
But the day when I rose at dawn from the bed of perfect health,
    refresh'd, singing, inhaling the ripe breath of autumn,
When I saw the full moon in the west grow pale and
    disappear in the morning light,

When I wander'd alone over the beach, and undressing bathed,
   laughing with the cool waters, and saw the sun rise,
And when I thought how my dear friend my lover was
   on his way coming, O then I was happy,
O then each breath tasted sweeter, and all that day my food
   nourish'd me more, and the beautiful day pass'd well,
And the next came with equal joy, and with the next at evening
   came my friend,
And that night while all was still I heard the waters roll slowly
   continually up the shores,
I heard the hissing rustle of the liquid and sands as directed to me
   whispering to congratulate me,
For the one I love most lay sleeping by me under the same cover
   in the cool night,
In the stillness in the autumn moonbeams his face was inclined
   towards me,
And his arm lay lightly around my breast – and that night I was
   happy.

WALT WHITMAN

Song

Lovely kind and kindly loving,
Such a mind were worth the moving:
Truly fair and fairly true –
Where are all these but in you?

Wisely kind and kindly wise,
Blessèd life, where such love lies!
Wise, and kind, and fair, and true –
Lovely live all these in you.

Sweetly dear and dearly sweet,
Blessèd where these blessings meet!
Sweet, fair, wise, kind, blessèd true –
Blessèd be all these in you!

NICHOLAS BRETON

To Celia

Drink to me only with thine eyes,
    And I will pledge with mine;
Or leave a kiss but in the cup,
    And I'll not look for wine.
The thirst that from the soul doth rise
    Doth ask a drink divine;
But might I of Jove's nectar sup,
    I would not change for thine.

I sent thee late a rosy wreath,
    Not so much honouring thee
As giving it a hope that there
    It could not withered be:
But thou thereon didst only breathe
    And sent'st it back to me;
Since when it grows, and smells, I swear,
    Not of itself, but thee!

BEN JONSON

I Will Make You Brooches

I will make you brooches and toys for your delight
Of bird-song at morning and star-shine at night.
I will make a palace fit for you and me
Of green days in forests and blue days at sea.

I will make my kitchen, and you shall keep your room,
Where white flows the river and bright blows the broom,
And you shall wash your linen and keep your body white
In rainfall at morning and dewfall at night.

And this shall be for music when no one else is near,
The fine song for singing, the rare song to hear!
That only I remember, that only you admire,
Of the broad road that stretches and the roadside fire.

ROBERT LOUIS STEVENSON

If Thou Must Love Me

SONNET FROM THE PORTUGUESE XIV

If thou must love me, let it be for nought
Except for love's sake only. Do not say
"I love her for her smile . . her look . . her way
Of speaking gently, . . for a trick of thought
That falls in well with mine and certes brought
A sense of pleasant ease on such a day" —
For these things in themselves, Beloved, may
Be changed, or change for thee, — and love so wrought,
May be unwrought so. Neither love me for
Thine own dear pity's wiping my cheeks dry,
Since one might well forget to weep who bore
Thy comfort long, and lose thy love thereby.
But love me for love's sake, that evermore
Thou may'st love on through love's eternity.

ELIZABETH BARRETT BROWNING

Dear If You Change! I'll Never Choose Again

Dear, if you change! I'll never choose again.
Sweet, if you shrink! I'll never think of love
Fair, if you fail! I'll judge all beauty vain.
Wise, if too weak! more wits I'll never prove.
      Dear! sweet! fair! wise! change, shrink, nor be not weak;
      And, on my faith! my faith shall never break.

Earth with her flowers shall sooner heaven adorn;
Heaven her bright stars, through earth's dim globe shall move.
Fire, heat shall lose; and frosts, of flames be born;
Air, made to shine, as black as hell shall prove;
      Earth, heaven, fire, air, the world transformed shall view,
      Ere I prove false to faith, or strange to you!

JOHN DOWLAND

A Woman's Reason

Love not me for comely grace,
    For my pleasing eye or face,
Nor for any outward part,
No, nor for a constant heart!
    For these may fail or turn to ill,
        So thou and I shall sever:
Keep, therefore, a true woman's eye,
And love me still but know not why!
    So hast thou the same reason still
        To dote upon me ever.

ANONYMOUS

The Passionate Shepherd To His Love

Come live with me, and be my love,
And we will all the pleasures prove
That valleys, groves, and hills, and fields,
Woods or steepy mountain yields.

And we will sit upon the rocks,
Seeing the shepherds feed their flocks
By shallow rivers, to whose falls
Melodious birds sing madrigals.

And I will make thee beds of roses,
And a thousand fragrant posies:
A cap of flowers, and a kirtle,
Embroidered all with leaves of myrtle.

A gown made of the finest wool,
Which from our pretty lambs we'll pull;
Fair linèd slippers for the cold,
With buckles of the purest gold.

CHRISTOPHER MARLOWE

The Garden

My heart shall be thy garden. Come my own,
Into thy garden; thine be happy hours
Among my fairest thoughts, my tallest flowers,
From root to crowning petal thine alone.
Thine is the place, from where the seeds are sown
Up to the sky enclosed, with all its showers.
But ah, the birds, the birds! Who shall build bowers
To keep these thine? O friend, the birds have flown.
For as these come and go, and quit our pine
To follow the sweet season, or, new-comers,
Sing one song only from our alder-trees,
My heart has thoughts, which, though thine eyes hold mine,
Flit to the silent world and other summers,
With wings that dip beyond the silver seas.

ALICE MEYNELL

My Sweetest Lesbia

My sweetest Lesbia, let us live and love;
And, though the sager sorts our deeds reprove,
Let us not weigh them: Heaven's great lamps do dive
Into their west, and straight again revive,
    But soon as once is set our little light
    Then must we sleep our ever-during night.

If all would lead their lives in love like me,
The bloody swords and armour should not be . . .
No drum nor trumpet peaceful sleeps should move,
Unless alarm came from the camp of love.
But fools do live, and waste their little light,
And seek with pain their ever-during night.

When timely death my life and fortune ends,
Let not my hearse be vexed with mourning friends,
But let all lovers, rich in triumph, come,
And with sweet pastimes grace my happy tomb;
And, Lesbia, close up thou my little light,
And crown with love my ever-during night.

THOMAS CAMPION

Love Me Little, Love Me Long

You say, to me-wards your affection's strong;
Pray love me little, so you love me long.
Slowly goes far; the mean is best: desire
Grown violent, does either die, or tire.

ROBERT HERRICK

To A Lady Asking How Long
He Would Love Her

It is not, Celia, in our power
    To say how long our love will last;
It may be we within this hour
    May lose those joys we now do taste;
The blessèd, that immortal be,
From change in love are only free.

Then since we mortal lovers are,
    Ask not how long our love will last;
But while it does, let us take care
    Each minute be with pleasure past:
Were it not madness to deny
To live because we're sure to die?

SIR GEORGE ETHEREGE

Face To Face

SONNET FROM THE PORTUGUESE XXII

When our two souls stand up erect and strong,
Face to face, silent, drawing nigh and nigher,
Until the lengthening wings break into fire
At either curving point, – what bitter wrong
Can the earth do us, that we should not long
Be here contented? Think! In mounting higher,
The angels would press on us, and aspire
To drop some golden orb of perfect song
Into our deep, dear silence. Let us stay
Rather on earth, belovèd – where the unfit
Contrarious moods of men recoil away
And isolate pure spirits, and permit
A place to stand and love in for a day,
With darkness and the death-hour rounding it.

ELIZABETH BARRETT BROWNING

Silent Is The House

(EXTRACT)

Come, the wind may never again
Blow as now it blows for us;
And the stars may never again shine
    as now they shine;
Long before October returns,
Seas of blood will have parted us:
And you must crush the love in your heart,
    and I the love in mine!

EMILY BRONTË

The Sleeper

Gazing down upon you I am made aware
Of your lost childhood; ere the grown years
Had brought me to wake your womanliness
Sleeping in beauty. How often thus had you lain
With one arm careless on the counterpane
And one curved back amongst your hair.
Innocence still lingers in the curl of a tress,
And in the little drooping mouth, and the cheek
Puffed up by the pillow. I could shed tears
Knowing that you must awake to endure
The conflict of the flesh in daily stress
Of wasting experiences; and yet my fears
Were greater thinking you might not awake.
Through what quiet continents of your own
Are you now walking, and with whom for a friend?
How often am I forgot when you are alone
Standing upon that ultimate verge of consciousness
Which sheers to death: each is alone at the end
And wearied of all this challengeable world
Ready to droop into oblivion
Like a sleepy child: thus, seeing your warm cheek
Pillowed so childlike I fain would bend
To kiss it but pity rebukes me.
Why should I hurry you back from yourself
Out of your created kingdom:
And yet, and yet, I stoop to your ear and speak
My name in whispers: I who can see
You sleeping serene in your own loneliness
And made aware of myself standing here
Within a loneliness more lone than sleep.

WILLIAM SOUTAR

The House Of Life

(EXTRACT)

Your hands lie open in the long fresh grass, –
The finger-points look through like rosy blooms:
Your eyes smile peace. The pasture gleams and glooms
'Neath billowing skies that scatter and amass.
All round our nest, far as the eye can pass,
Are golden kingcup-fields with silver edge
Where the cow-parsley skirts the hawthorn-hedge.
'Tis visible silence, still as the hour-glass.
Deep in the sun-searched growths the dragon-fly
Hangs like a blue thread loosened from the sky:–
So this winged hour is dropped to us from above.
Oh! clasp we to our hearts, for deathless dower,
This close-companioned inarticulate hour
When two-fold silence was the song of love.

DANTE GABRIEL ROSSETTI

Song

From THE PRINCESS

Now sleeps the crimson petal, now the white;
Nor waves the cypress in the palace walk;
Nor winks the gold fin in the porphyry font:
The firefly wakens: waken thou with me.

Now droops the milkwhite peacock like a ghost,
And like a ghost she glimmers on to me.

Now lies the earth all Danaë to the stars,
And all thy heart lies open unto me.

Now slides the silent meteor on, and leaves
A shining furrow, as thy thoughts in me.

Now folds the lily all her sweetness up,
And slips into the bosom of the lake:
So fold thyself, my dearest, thou, and slip
Into my bosom and be lost in me.

ALFRED, LORD TENNYSON

The Love I Bear Thee

SONNET FROM THE PORTUGUESE XIII

And wilt thou have me fashion into speech
The love I bear thee, finding words enough,
And hold the torch out, while the winds are rough,
Between our faces, to cast light on each?
I drop it at thy feet. I cannot teach
My hand to hold my spirit so far off
From myself . . me . . that I should bring thee proof
In words, of love hid in me out of reach.
Nay, let the silence of my womanhood
Commend my woman-love to thy belief, –
Seeing that I stand unwon, however wooed,
And rend the garment of my life, in brief,
By a most dauntless, voiceless fortitude,
Let one touch of this heart convey its grief.

ELIZABETH BARRETT BROWNING

Song

Dear Colin, prevent my warm blushes,
    Since how can I speak without pain?
My eyes have oft told you my wishes,
    Oh! can't you their meaning explain?

My passion would lose by expression,
　　And you too might cruelly blame;
Then don't you expect a confession
　　Of what is too tender to name.

Since yours is the province of speaking,
　　Why should you expect it from me?
Our wishes should be in our keeping,
　　Till you tell us what they should be.

Then quickly why don't you discover?
　　Did your heart feel such tortures as mine,
Eyes need not tell over and over
　　What I in my bosom confine.

LADY MARY WORTLEY MONTAGU

Unto The Boundless Ocean Of Thy Beauty

Unto the boundless ocean of thy beauty,
Runs this poor river, charged with streams of zeal
Returning thee the tribute of my duty,
Which here my love, my youth, my plaints reveal.
Here I unclasp the book of my charg'd soul,
Where I have cast th'accounts of all my care:
Here have I summ'd my sighs; here I enroll
How they were spent for thee; look what they are,
Look on the dear expenses of my youth,
And see how just I reckon with thine eyes:
Examine well thy beauty with my truth;
And cross my cares, ere greater sums arise.
　　Read it, sweet maid, tho' it be done but slightly;
　　Who can show all his love, doth love but lightly.

SAMUEL DANIEL

Vision

To-day there have been lovely things
I never saw before;
Sunlight through a jar of marmalade;
A blue gate;
A rainbow
In soapsuds on dishwater;
Candlelight on butter;
The crinkled smile of a little girl
Who had new shoes with tassels;
A chickadee on a thorn-apple;
Empurpled mud under a willow,
Where white geese slept;
White ruffled curtains sifting moonlight
On the scrubbed kitchen floor;
The under-side of a white-oak leaf;
Ruts in the road at sunset;
An egg yolk in a blue bowl.

My love kissed my eyes last night.

MAY THIELGAARD WATTS

The Great Lover

I have been so great a lover: filled my days
So proudly with the splendour of love's praise,
The pain, the calm, and the astonishment,
Desire illimitable, and still content,
And all dear names men use, to cheat despair
For the perplexed and viewless streams that bear
Our hearts at random down the dark of life.
Now, ere the unthinking silence on that strife
Steals down, I would cheat drowsy death so far,
My night shall be remembered for a star
That outshone all the suns of all men's days.

Shall I not crown them with immortal praise
Whom I have loved, who have given me, dared with me
High secrets, and in darkness knelt to see
The inenarrable godhead of delight?
Love is a flame: – we have beaconed the world's night.
A city: – and we have built it, these and I.
An emperor: – we have taught the world to die.
So, for their sakes I loved, ere I go hence,
And the high cause of love's magnificence,
And to keep loyalties young, I'll write those names
Golden for ever, eagles, crying flames,
And set them as a banner, that men may know.
To dare the generations, burn, and blow
Out on the wind of time, shining and streaming . . .

These I have loved:
                        White plates and cups, clean-gleaming,
Ringed with blue lines; and feathery, faery dust;
Wet roofs, beneath the lamp-light; the strong crust
Of friendly bread; and many-tasting food;
Rainbows; and the blue bitter smoke of wood;
And radiant raindrops couching in cool flowers;
And flowers themselves, that sway through sunny hours,
Dreaming of moths that drink them under the moon;
Then, the cool kindliness of sheets, that soon
Smooth away trouble; and the rough male kiss
Of blankets; grainy wood; live hair that is
Shining and free; blue-massing clouds; the keen
Unpassioned beauty of a great machine;
The benison of hot water; furs to touch;
The good smell of old clothes; and other such –
The comfortable smell of friendly fingers,
Hair's fragrance, and the musty reek that lingers
About dead leaves and last year's ferns . . .
                                          Dear names,
And thousand other throng to me! Royal flames;
Sweet water's dimpling laugh from tap or spring;
Holes in the ground; and voices that do sing;
Voices in laughter, too; and body's pain,
Soon turned to peace; and the deep-panting train;

Firm sands; the little dulling edge of foam
That browns and dwindles as the wave goes home;
And washen stones, gay for an hour; the cold
Graveness of iron; moist black earthen mould;
Sleep; and high places; footprints in the dew;
And oaks; and brown horse-chestnuts, glossy-new;
And new-peeled sticks; and shining pools on grass; —
All these have been my loves. And these shall pass,
Whatever passes not, in the great hour,
Nor all my passion, all my prayers, have power
To hold them with me through the gate of death.
They'll play deserter, turn with the traitor breath,
Break the high bond we made, and sell love's trust
And sacramented covenant to the dust.
— Oh, never a doubt but, somewhere, I shall wake,
And give what's left of love again; and make
New friends, now strangers . . .
                              But the best I've known,
Stays here, and changes, breaks, grows old, is blown
About the winds of the world, and fades from brains
Of living men, and dies.
                              Nothing remains

O dear my loves, O faithless, once again
This one last gift I give: that after men
Shall know, and later lovers, far removed,
Praise you, 'All these were lovely'; say, 'He loved.'

RUPERT BROOKE

Driftwood

My forefathers gave me
    My spirit's shaken flame
The shape of hands, the beat of heart,
    The letters of my name.

But it was my lovers,
   And not my sleeping sires,
Who gave the flame its changeful
   And iridescent fires;

As the driftwood burning
   Took its jewelled blaze
From the sea's blue splendour
   Of coloured nights and days.

            SARA TEASDALE

Two In The Campagna

(EXTRACT)

I would I could adopt your will,
   See with your eyes, and set my heart
Beating by yours and drink my fill
   At your soul's springs, – your part my part
In life, for good and ill.

No. I yearn upward, touch you close,
   Then stand away. I kiss your cheek,
Catch your soul's warmth, – I pluck the rose
   And love it more than tongue can speak –
Then the good minute goes.

Already how am I so far
   Out of that minute? Must I go
Still like the thistle-ball, no bar,
   Onward, whenever light winds blow,
Fixed by no friendly star?

Just when I seemed about to learn!
   Where is the thread now? Off again!
The old trick! Only I discern –
   Infinite passion, and the pain
Of finite hearts that yearn.

            ROBERT BROWNING

To –

One word is too often profaned
   For me to profane it,
One feeling too falsely disdained
   For thee to disdain it;
One hope is too like despair
   For prudence to smother,
And pity from thee more dear
   Than that from another.

I can give not what men call love,
   But wilt thou accept not
The worship the heart lifts above
   And the heavens reject not, –
The desire of the moth for the star,
   Of the night for the morrow,
The devotion to something afar
   From the sphere of our sorrow?

PERCY BYSSHE SHELLEY

'Tis All That Heaven Allows

All my past life is mine no more;
   The flying hours are gone,
Like transitory dreams given o'er
Whose images are kept in store
   By memory alone.

Whatever is to come is not:
   How can it then be mine?
The present moment's all my lot,
And that, as fast as it is got,
   Phyllis, is wholly thine.

Then talk not of inconstancy,
    False hearts, and broken vows;
If I, by miracle, can be
This livelong minute true to thee,
    'Tis all that heaven allows.

JOHN WILMOT, EARL OF ROCHESTER

To One That Asked Me Why I Loved J.G.

Why do I love? Go, ask the glorious sun
Why every day it round the world doth run;
Ask Thames and Tiber, why they ebb and flow:
Ask damask roses why in June they blow:
Ask ice and hail the reason why they're cold:
Decaying beauties, why they will grow old
They'll tell thee, fate, that every thing doth move,
Inforces them to this, and me to love,
There is no reason for our love or hate;
'Tis irresistible, as death or fate;
'Tis not his face; I've sense enough to see,
That is not good, though doated on by me;
Nor is't his tongue, that has this conquest won;
For that at least is equall'd by my own:
His carriage can to none obliging be,
'Tis rude, affected, full of vanity:
Strangely ill-natured, peevish and unkind,
Unconstant, false, to jealousy inclined,
His temper could not have so great a power,
'Tis mutable, and changes every hour:
Those vigorous years that women so adore,
Are past in him: he's twice my age, and more;
And yet I love this false, this worthless man
With all the passion that a woman can;
Doat on his imperfections, though I spy
Nothing to love; I love, and know not why.

Since 'tis decreed in the dark book of fate
That I should love, and he should be ingrate.

'EPHELIA'

How Do I Love Thee?

SONNET FROM THE PORTUGUESE XLII

How do I love thee? Let me count the ways.
I love thee to the depth, and breadth, and height
My soul can reach, when feeling out of sight
For the ends of being and ideal grace.
I love thee to the level of every day's
Most quiet need, by sun and candlelight.
I love thee freely, as men strive for right:
I love thee purely, as they turn from praise.
I love thee with the passion put to use
In my old griefs, and with my childhood's faith.
I love thee with a love I seemed to lose
With my lost saints. I love thee with the breath,
Smiles, tears, of all my life — and if God choose,
I shall but love thee better after death.

ELIZABETH BARRETT BROWNING

Song

Say what is love – to live in vain
To live and die and live again

Say what is love – is it to be
In prison still and still be free

Or seem as free – alone and prove
The hopeless hopes of real love?

Does real love on earth exist?
'Tis like a sunbeam on the mist

That fades and nowhere will remain
And nowhere is o'ertook again.

Say what is love – a blooming name
A rose leaf on the page of fame

That blooms then fades – to cheat no more
And is what nothing was before.

Say what is love – what e'er it be
It centres, Mary, still with thee.

JOHN CLARE

Why Do I Love Her?

'Tis not her birth, her friends, nor yet her treasure,
Nor do I covet her for sensual pleasure,
Nor for that old morality
Do I love her, 'cause she loves me.
Sure he that loves his lady 'cause she's fair,
Delights his eye, so loves himself, not her.
Something there is moves me to love, and I
Do know I love, but know not how, nor why.

ALEXANDER BROME

The Je Ne Sais Quoi

Yes, I'm in love, I feel it now,
    And Celia has undone me;
And yet I'll swear I can't tell how
    The pleasing plague stole on me.

'Tis not her face that love creates,
  For there no graces revel;
'Tis not her shape, for there the fates
  Have rather been uncivil.

'Tis not her shape, for sure in that,
  There's nothing more than common;
And all her sense is only chat,
  Like any other woman.

Her voice, her touch, might give the alarm —
  'Tis both perhaps, or neither;
In short, 'tis that provoking charm
  Of Celia altogether.

                                WILLIAM WHITEHEAD

I Do Not Love Thee

I do not love thee! No! I do not love thee!
And yet when thou art absent I am sad;
And envy even the bright blue sky above thee,
Whose quiet stars may see thee and be glad.

I do not love thee! yet, I know not why,
Whate'er thou does seems still well done, to me —
And often in my solitude I sigh —
That those I do love are not more like thee!

I do not love thee! yet when thou art gone
I hate the sound (though those who speak be dear)
Which breaks the lingering echo of the tone
Thy voice of music leaves upon my ear.

I do not love thee! yet thy speaking eyes,
With their deep, bright and most expressive blue —
Between me and the midnight heaven arise,
Oftener than any eyes I ever knew.

I know I do not love thee! yet, alas!
Others will scarcely trust my candid heart;
And oft I catch them smiling as they pass,
Because they see me gazing where thou art.

CAROLINE NORTON

Love's Story

I do not love thee,
So I'll not deceive thee.
I do not love thee,
Yet I'm loth to leave thee.

I do not love thee,
Yet joy's very essence
Comes with thy footstep,
Is complete in thy presence.

I do not love thee,
Yet when gone I sigh
And think about thee
'Till the stars all die.

I do not love thee,
Yet thy black bright eyes
Bring to my heart's soul
Heaven and paradise.

I do not love thee,
Yet thy handsome ways
Bring me in absence
Almost hopeless days.

I cannot hate thee,
Yet my love seems debtor
To love thee more
So hating, love thee better.

JOHN CLARE

One Day I Wrote Her Name Upon the Strand

One day I wrote her name upon the strand,
    But came the waves and washèd it away:
Again I wrote it with a second hand,
    But came the tide, and made my pains his prey.
'Vain man,' said she, 'thou dost in vain assay,
    A mortal thing so to immortalize,
For I myself shall like to this decay,
    And eek my name be wipèd out likewise.'
'Not so,' quoth I, 'let baser things devise
    To die in dust, but you shall live by fame:
My verse your virtues rare shall eternise,
    And in the heavens write your glorious name,
        Where, whenas death shall all the world subdue,
        Our love shall live, and later life renew.'

EDMUND SPENSER

Song

From SYLVA

The streams that wind amid the hills,
    And lost in pleasure slowly roam,
While their deep joy the valley fills, –
    Ev'n these will leave their mountain-home:
    So may it, love! with others be,
    But I will never wend from thee!

The leaf forsakes the parent spray,
    The blossom quits the stem as fast,
The rose-enamoured bird will stray,
    And leave his eglantine at last;
    So may it, love! with others be,
    But I will never wend from thee!

GEORGE DARLEY

THE NATURE OF LOVE

Love Is The Heaven's Fair Aspect

From THE SHEPHERD'S GARLAND

Love is the heaven's fair aspect,
    love is the glory of the earth,
Love only doth our lives direct,
    love is our guider from our birth.

Love taught my thoughts at first to fly,
    love taught mine eyes the way to love,
Love raisèd my conceit so high,
    love framed my hand his art to prove.

Love taught my muse her perfect skill
    love gave me first to poesy:
Love is the sovereign of my will,
    love bound me first to loyalty.

Love was the first that framed my speech,
    love was the first that gave me grace:
Love is my life and fortune's leech,
    love made the virtuous give me place.

Love is the end of my desire,
    love is the lodestar of my love,
Love makes my self, my self admire,
    love seated my delights above.

Love placèd honour in my breast,
    love made me learning's favourite,
Love made me likèd of the best,
    love first my mind on virtue set.

Love is my life, life is my love,
    love is my whole felicity,
Love is my sweet, sweet is my love,
    I am in love, and love in me.

MICHAEL DRAYTON

Song

O love, that stronger art than wine,
Pleasing delusion, witchery divine,
Wont to be prized above all wealth,
Disease that has more joys than health,
Tho' we blaspheme thee in our pain
And of thy tyranny complain,
We all are bettered by thy reign.
What reason never can bestow
We to this useful passion owe:
Love wakes the dull from sluggish ease,
And learns a clown the art to please,
Humbles the vain, kindles the cold,
Makes misers free and cowards bold;
'Tis he reforms the sot from drink,
And teaches airy fops to think.
When full brute appetite is fed,
And choked the glutton lies and dead,
Thou new spirits dost dispense
And 'finest the gross delights of sense:
Virtue's unconquerable aid
That against nature can persuade,
And mak'st a roving mind retire
Within the bounds of just desire;
Cheerer of age, youth's kind unrest,
And half the heaven of the blest!

APHRA BEHN

Love Comforteth Like Sunshine After Rain

From VENUS AND ADONIS

Love comforteth like sunshine after rain,
But lust's effect is tempest after sun;
Love's gentle spring doth always fresh remain,
Lust's winter comes ere summer half be done;
  Love surfeits not; lust like a glutton dies;
  Love is all truth; lust full of forgèd lies.' . . .

WILLIAM SHAKESPEARE

The Most Generous Passion

Love, the most generous passion of the mind,
The softest refuge innocence can find;
The safe director of misguided youth,
Fraught with kind wishes, and secur'd by truth;
The cordial drop heaven in our cup has thrown,
To make the nauseous draught of life go down;
On which one only blessing God might raise,
In lands of atheists, subsidies of praise;
For none did e'er so dull and stupid prove,
But felt a god, and bless'd his power in love.

JOHN WILMOT, EARL OF ROCHESTER

A Soft Divinity

– There is in love a power,
There is a soft divinity that draws transport
Even from distress; that gives the heart
A certain pang, excelling far the joys
Of gross unfeeling life.

DAVID MALLET

A Song

Love, thou art best of human joys,
   Our chiefest happiness below;
All other pleasures are but toys,
Music without thee is but noise,
     And beauty but an empty show.

Heaven, who knew best what man would move,
   And raise his thoughts above the brute;
Said, Let him Be, and Let him Love;
That must alone his soul improve,
     Howe'er philosophers dispute.

ANN FINCH

Pastiche

Love, oh, love's a dainty sweeting,
Wooing now, and now retreating;
Brightest joy and blackest care,
Swift as light, and light as air.

Would you seize and fix and capture
All his evanescent rapture?
Bind him fast with golden curls,
Fetter with a chain of pearls?

Would you catch him in a net,
Like a white moth prankt with jet?
Clutch him, and his bloomy wing
Turns a dead, discoloured thing!

Pluck him like a rosebud red,
And he leaves a thorn instead;
Let him go without a care,
And he follows unaware.

Love, oh, Love's a dainty sweeting,
Wooing now, and now retreating;
Lightly come, and lightly gone,
Lost when most securely won!

MATHILDE BLIND

Paradox. That Fruition Destroys Love

(EXTRACT)

. . . Since lovers' joys then leave so sick a taste,
And soon as relished by the sense are past;
They are but riddles sure, lost if possesed,
And therefore only in reversion best.
For bate them expectation and delay,
You take the most delightful scenes away.
These two such rule within the fancy keep,
As banquets apprehended in our sleep;
After which pleasing trance next morn we wake
Empty and angry at the night's mistake.
Give me long dreams and visions of content,
Rather than pleasures in a minute spent.
And since I know before, the shedding rose
In that same instant doth her sweetness lose,
Upon the virgin-stock still let her dwell
For me, to feast my longings with her smell.
Those are but counterfeits of joy at best,
Which languish soon as brought unto the test.
Nor can I hold it worth his pains who tries
To in that harvest which by reaping dies . . .
To close my argument then. I dare say
(And without paradox) as well we may
Enjoy our love and yet preserve desire,
As warm our hands by putting out the fire.

HENRY KING

Love

Love is begot by fancy, bred
   By ignorance, by expectation fed,
Destroyed by knowledge, and, at best,
Lost in the moment 'tis possessed.

GEORGE GRANVILLE, BARON LANSDOWNE

No Platonic Love

Tell me no more of minds embracing minds,
   And hearts exchanged for hearts;
That spirits spirits meet, as winds do winds,
   And mix their subt'lest parts;
That two unbodied essences may kiss,
And then like angels, twist and feel one bliss.

I was that silly thing that once was wrought
   To practise this thin love;
I climbed from sex to soul, from soul to thought;
   But thinking there to move,
Headlong I rolled from thought to soul, and then
From soul I lighted at the sex again.

As some strict down-looked men pretend to fast,
   Who yet in closets eat;
So lovers who profess they spirits taste,
   Feed yet on grosser meat;
I know they boast they souls to souls convey.
Howe'r they meet, the body is the way.

Come, I will undeceive thee, they that tread
   Those vain aerial ways,
Are like young heirs and alchemists misled
   To waste their wealth and days,
For searching thus to be for ever rich,
They only find a med'cine for the itch.

WILLIAM CARTWRIGHT

Love's Trinity

Soul, heart, and body, we thus singly name,
　　Are not in love divisible and distinct,
　　But each with each inseparably link'd.
　One is not honour, and the other shame,
But burn as closely fused as fuel, heat, and flame.

They do not love who give the body and keep
　　The heart ungiven; nor they who yield the soul,
　　And guard the body. Love doth give the whole;
　Its range being high as heaven, as ocean deep,
Wide as the realms of air or planet's curving sweep.

ALFRED AUSTIN

Love Is Ever A Mixed Sense

From CHORUS

　. . . Doth not our chiefest bliss then lie
　Betwixt thirst and satiety,
　In the midway: which is alone
　In an half-satisfaction:
　And is not love the middle way,
　At which with most delight we stay;
　Desire is total indigence,
　But love is ever a mixed sense
　Of what we have, and what we want,
　And though it be a little scant
　Of satisfaction, yet we rest
　In such an half-possession best.
　A half-possession doth supply
　The pleasure of variety,
　And frees us from inconstancy
　By want caused, or satiety;

He never loved, who doth confess
He wanted aught he doth possess,
(Love to itself is recompense
Besides the pleasure of the sense).

SIDNEY GODOLPHIN

What Thing Is Love?

What thing is love? for sure love is a thing.
It is a prick, it is a sting,
It is a pretty, pretty thing;
It is a fire, it is a coal,
Whose flame creeps in at every hole;
And as my wit doth best devise,
Love's dwelling is in ladies' eyes,
From whence do glance love's piercing darts,
That make such holes into our hearts;
And all the world herein accord,
Love is a great and mighty lord;
And when he list to mount so high,
With Venus he in heaven doth lie,
And evermore hath been a god,
Since Mars and she played even and odd.

GEORGE PEELE

Love

Love is anterior to life,
        Posterior to death,
Initial of creation, and
        The exponent of breath.

EMILY DICKINSON

Love

Love bade me welcome: yet my soul drew back,
    Guilty of dust and sin.
But quick-eyed Love, observing me grow slack
    From my first entrance in,
Drew nearer to me, sweetly questioning,
    If I lacked any thing.

'A guest,' I answered, 'worthy to be here:'
    Love said, 'You shall be he.'
'I the unkind, ungrateful? Ah my dear,
    I cannot look on Thee.'
Love took my hand, and smiling did reply,
    'Who made the eyes but I?'

'Truth Lord, but I have marred them: let my shame
    Go where it doth deserve.'
'And know you not,' says Love, 'Who bore the blame?'
    'My dear, then I will serve.'
'You must sit down,' says Love, 'and taste my meat:'
    So I did sit and eat.

GEORGE HERBERT

Love Is Like A Dizziness

O, love, love, love!
    Love is like a dizziness;
It winna let a poor body
    Gang about his biziness!

JAMES HOGG

Of Love. A Sonnet

How love came in, I do not know,
Whether by th'eye, or ear, or no:
Or whether with the soul it came
(At first) infused with the same:
Whether in part 'tis here or there,
Or, like the soul, whole everywhere:
This troubles me: but I as well
As any other, this can tell;
That when from hence she does depart,
The out-let then is from the heart.

ROBERT HERRICK

The Divorce Of Sense And Reason

Love is a law, a discord of such force
That 'twixt our sense and reason makes divorce.
Love's a desire that to obtain betime
We lose an age of years pluck'd from our prime,
Love is a thing to which we soon consent,
As soon refuse, but sooner far repent.
Then what must women be that are the cause,
That love hath life? that lovers feel such laws?
They're like the winds upon Lapanthae's shores,
That still are changing. Oh then love no more.
A woman's love is like that Syrian flow'r
That buds and spreads, and withers in an hour.

ANONYMOUS

Never Sick, Never Dead, Never Cold

Know that love is a careless child,
    And forgets promise past:
He is blind, he is deaf when he list,
    And in faith never fast.

His desire is a dureless content,
    And a trustless joy;
He is won with a world of despair,
    And is lost with a toy.

Of womenkind such indeed is the love,
    Or the word love abusèd,
Under which many childish desires
    And conceits are excusèd.

But true love is a durable fire,
    In the mind ever burning,
Never sick, never dead, never cold,
    From itself never turning.

ANONYMOUS

The Fume Of Sighs

From ROMEO AND JULIET

Love is a smoke raised with the fume of sighs,
Being purged, a fire sparkling in lovers' eyes,
Being vexed, a sea nourished with lovers' tears.
What is it else? a madness, most discreet,
A choking gall, and a preserving sweet.

WILLIAM SHAKESPEARE

And This Is Love

A heat full of coldness, a sweet full of
Bitterness, a pain full of pleasantness,
Which maketh thoughts have eyes, and hearts,
And ears; bred by desire, nurs'd by delight,
Weaned by ingratitude: and this is love.

JOHN LYLY

Inordinate Love

I shall say what inordinat love is:
The furiosité and wodness* of minde,
A instinguible brenning† fawting blis,
A gret hungre, insaciat to finde,
A dowcet° ille, a ivell swetness blinde,
A right wonderfulle, sugred, swete errour,
Withoute labour rest, contrary to kinde•,
Or withoute quiete to have huge labour.

ANONYMOUS

*madness　　　　†burning　　　　°dulcet　　　　•nature

Love Is The Treacle Of Sin

Truth telleth thee that love is the treacle of sin,
A sovran salve for body and soul.
Love is the plant of peace, most precious of the virtues.
Heaven could not hold it, so heavy was love,
Till it has of this earth eaten its fill;
Then never lighter was a leaf upon a linden tree,
Than love was when it took the flesh and blood of man.
Fluttering, piercing as a needle's point,
No armour may it stay, nor no high walls.

WILLIAM LANGLAND

To The Queen

Our passions are most like to floods and streams;
The shallow murmur; but the deep are dumb.
So when affections yield discourse, it sees
The bottom is but shallow whence they come.
　　They that are rich in words must needs discover
　　That they are poor in that which makes a lover.

Wrong not, dear empress of my heart,
　　The merit of true passion,
With thinking that he feels no smart,
　　That sues for no compassion:
Since, if my plaints serve not to prove
　　The conquest of your beauty,
It comes not from defect of love,
　　But from excess of duty.

For knowing that I sue to serve
　　A saint of such perfection,
As all desire, but none deserve,
　　A place in her affection:
I rather choose to want relief
　　Than venture the revealing;
When glory recommends the grief,
　　Despair distrusts the healing.

Thus those desires that aim too high,
　　For any mortal lover,
When reason cannot make them die,
　　Discretion will them cover.
Yet when discretion doth bereave
　　The plaints that they should utter,
Then your discretion may perceive,
　　That silence is a suitor.

Silence in love bewrays* more woe,
    Than words, though ne'er so witty,
A beggar that is dumb, ye know,
    Deserveth double pity.
Then misconceive not (dearest heart)
    My true, though secret passion,
He smarteth most that hides his smart,
    And sues for no compassion.

                       SIR WALTER RALEGH

*reveals

She That Denies Me

She that denies me, I would have;
    Who craves me, I despise:
Venus hath power to rule mine heart,
    But not to please mine eyes.
Temptations offered, I still scorn;
    Denied, I cling them still:
I'll neither glut mine appetite,
    Nor seek to starve my will.

Diana, double-clothed, offends;
    So, Venus, naked quite:
The last begets a surfeit, and
    The other no delight.
That crafty girl shall please me best
    That other no delight.
That crafty girl shall please me best
    That *No*, for *Yea*, can say,
And every wanton willing kiss
    Can season with a *Nay*.

                    THOMAS HEYWOOD

Love Is Love, In Beggars And In Kings

From A POETICAL RHAPSODY

The lowest trees have tops, the ant her gall,
    The fly her spleen, the little spark his heat;
And slender hairs cast shadows, though but small,
    And bees have stings, although they be not great;
Seas have their source, and so have shallow springs;
And love is love, in beggars and in kings.
Where waters smoothest run, deep are the fords;
    The dial stirs, yet none perceives it move;
The firmest faith is in the fewest words;
    The turtles cannot sing, and yet they love;
True hearts have eyes and ears, no tongues to speak;
They hear, and see, and sigh, and then they break.

SIR EDWARD DYER

The Fountains Smoke

The fountains smoke, and yet no flames they show;
    Stars shine all night, though undiscerned by day;
And trees do spring, yet are not seen to grow;
    And shadows move, although they seem to stay.
      In winter's woe is buried summer's bliss,
      And Love loves most where Love most secret is.

The stillest streams descry the greatest deep;
    The clearest sky is subject to a shower;
Conceit's most sweet whenas it seems to sleep;
    And fairest days do in the morning lower.
      The silent grove sweet nymphs they cannot miss,
      For Love loves most where Love most secret is.

The rarest jewels hidden virtue yield;
  The sweet of traffic is a secret gain;
The year once old doth show a barren field;
  And plants seem dead, and yet they spring again:
    Cupid is blind: the reason why is this:
    Love loveth most where Love most secret is.

ANONYMOUS

A Lover's Ear Will Hear The Lowest Sound

From LOVE'S LABOUR'S LOST

A lover's eyes will gaze an eagle blind,
A lover's ear will hear the lowest sound,
When the suspicious head of theft is stopped.
Love's feeling is more soft and sensible
Than are the tender horns of cockled snails.
Love's tongue proves dainty Bacchus gross in taste.
For valour, is not Love a Hercules,
Still climbing trees in the Hesperides?
Subtle as Sphinx; as sweet and musical
As bright Apollo's lute, strung with his hair.
And when Love speaks, the voice of all the gods
Makes heaven drowsy with the harmony.
Never durst poet touch a pen to write
Until his ink were temp'red with Love's sighs;
O then his lines would ravish savage ears
And plant in tyrants mild humility,
From women's eyes this doctrine I derive.
They sparkle still the right Promethean fire;
They are the books, the arts, the academes,
That show, contain, and nourish all the world.

WILLIAM SHAKESPEARE

No Thing Is To Man So Dear

No thyng ys to man so dere
As wommanys love in good manere.
A gode woman is mannys blys,
There her love right and stedfast ys.
There ys no solas under hevene
Of alle that a man may nevene*
That shulde a man so moche glew†
As a gode woman that loveth true.
Ne derer is none in Goddis hurde°
Than a chaste womman with lovely worde●.

ROBERT MANNYNG

*tell   †please   °treasury   ●good repute

Give All To Love

Give all to love;
Obey thy heart;
Friends, kindred, days,
Estate, good fame,
Plans, credit, and the Muse –
Nothing refuse.

'Tis a brave master;
Let it have scope:
Follow it utterly,
Hope beyond hope:
High and more high
It dives into noon,
With wing unspent,
Untold intent;
But it is a god,
Knows its own path,
And the outlets of the sky.

It was never for the mean;
It requireth courage stout,
Souls above doubt,
Valour unbending:
Such 'twill reward; –
They shall return
More than they were,
And ever ascending.

Leave all for love;
Yet, hear me, yet,
One word more thy heart beloved,
One pulse more of firm endeavour –
Keep thee to-day,
To-morrow, for ever,
Free as an Arab
Of thy beloved.

Cling with life to the maid;
But when the surprise,
First vague shadow of surmise,
Flits across her bosom young,
Of a joy apart from thee,
Free be she, fancy-free;
Nor thou detain her vesture's hem,
Nor the palest rose she flung
From her summer diadem.

Though thou loved her as thyself,
As a self of purer clay;
Though her parting dims the day,
Stealing grace from all alive;
Heartily know,
When half-gods go
The gods arrive.

RALPH WALDO EMERSON

IN PRAISE OF THE BELOVED

Shall I Compare Thee?

Shall I compare thee to a summer's day?
  Thou art more lovely and more temperate:
Rough winds do shake the darling buds of May,
  And summer's lease hath all too short a date:
Sometime too hot the eye of heaven shines,
  And often is his gold complexion dimmed;
And every fair from fair sometime declines,
  By chance, or nature's changing course untrimmed;
But thy eternal summer shall not fade,
  Nor lose possession of that fair thou owest,
Nor shall death brag thou wanderest in his shade,
  When in eternal lines to time thou growest;
    So long as men can breathe, or eyes can see,
    So long lives this, and this gives life to thee.

WILLIAM SHAKESPEARE

A Red, Red Rose

O my luve is like a red, red rose
  That's newly sprung in June.
O, my luve is like the melodie,
  That's sweetly play'd in tune.

As fair art thou, my bonnie lass,
  So deep in luve am I,
And I will luve thee still, my dear,
  Till a' the seas gang dry.

Till a' the seas gang dry, my dear,
    And the rocks melt wi' the sun!
And I will love thee still, my dear,
    While the sands o' life shall run.

And fare thee weel, my only luve,
    And fare thee weel a while!
And I will come again, my luve,
    Tho it were ten thousand mile!

ROBERT BURNS

She Walks In Beauty

She walks in beauty, like the night
    Of cloudless climes and starry skies;
And all that's best of dark and bright
    Meet in her aspect and her eyes:
Thus mellowed to that tender light
    Which heaven to gaudy day denies.

One shade the more, one ray the less,
    Had half impaired the nameless grace
Which waves in every raven tress,
    Or softly lightens o'er her face;
Where thoughts serenely sweet express
    How pure, how dear their dwelling-place.

And on that cheek, and o'er that brow,
    So soft, so calm, yet eloquent,
The smiles that win, the tints that glow,
    But tell of days in goodness spent,
A mind at peace with all below,
    A heart whose love is innocent!

GEORGE GORDON, LORD BYRON

Sonnet

Oh! death will find me, long before I tire
   Of watching you; and swing me suddenly
Into the shade and loneliness and mire
   Of the last land! There, waiting patiently,

One day, I think, I'll feel a cool wind blowing,
   See a slow light across the Stygian tide,
And hear the dead about me stir, unknowing,
   And tremble. And I shall know that you have died.

And watch you, a broad-browed and smiling dream,
   Pass, light as ever, through the lightless host,
Quietly ponder, start, and sway, and gleam –
   Most individual and bewildering ghost! –

And turn, and toss your brown delightful head
Amusedly, among the ancient dead.

RUPERT BROOKE

In Celebration Of Charis

(EXTRACT)

. . . Do but look on her eyes, they do light
All that love's world compriseth!
Do but look on her hair, it is bright
As love's star, when it riseth!
Do but mark, her forehead's smoother
   Than words that soothe her;
And from her arched brows such a grace
   Sheds itself through the face,
As alone there triumphs to the life
All the gain, all the good, of the elements' strife.

Have you seen but a bright lily grow
Before rude hands have touched it?
Have you marked but the fall o' the snow
Before the soil hath smutched it?
Have you felt the wool of the beaver,
    Or swan's down ever?
Or have smelt o' the bud o' the brier,
    Or the nard in the fire?
Or have tasted the bag of the bee?
O so white, O so soft, O so sweet is she!

BEN JONSON

Father And Child

She hears me strike the board and say
That she is under ban
Of all good men and women,
Being mentioned with a man
That has the worst of all bad names;
And there-upon replies
That his hair is beautiful,
Cold as the March wind his eyes.

W.B. YEATS

The Legend Of Good Women

(EXTRACT)

. . . She is the clernesse and the verray light,
That in this derké worlde me wynt and ledeth,
The herte in-with my sorowful brest yow dredeth,
And loveth so sore, that ye ben verrayly
The maistresse of my wit, and nothing I.
My word, my werk, is knit so in your bonde,
That, as an harpe obeyeth to the honde

And maketh hit soune after his fingeringe,
Right so mowe ye out of myn herté bringe
Swich vois, right as yow list, to laughe or pleyne.
Be ye my gyde and lady sovereyne;
As to myn erthly god, to yow I calle,
Bothe in this werke and in my sorwés alle . . .

GEOFFREY CHAUCER

My Lady

I loved her for that she was beautiful;
And that to me she seem'd to be all Nature,
And all varieties of things in one:
Would set at night in clouds of tears, and rise
All light and laughter in the morning; fear
No petty customs nor appearances;
But think what others only dream'd about;
And say what others did but think; and do
What others dared but do: so pure withal
In soul; in heart and act such conscious yet
Such perfect innocence, she made round her
A halo of delight. 'Twas these which won me; –
And that she never school'd within her breast
One thought or feeling, but gave holiday
To all; and that she made all even mine
In the communion of love: and we
Grew like each other, for we loved each other;
She, mild and generous as the air in spring;
And I, like earth all budding out with love.

PHILIP JAMES BAILEY

That Field Of Love

I saw her stretched upon a flow'ry bank,
With her soft sorrows lulled into a slumber:
The summer's heat had to her nat'ral blush
Added a brighter and more tempting red:
The beauties of her neck, and naked breasts,
Lifted by inward starts, did rise and fall,
With motion that might put a soul in statue;
The matchless whiteness of her folded arms,
That seemed t'embrace the body whence they grew,
Fix'd me to gaze o'er all that field of love.
While to my ravished eyes officious wind,
Waving her robes, display'd such well turned limbs
As artists would in polished marble give
The wanton goddess, when supinely laid
She charms her gallant god to new enjoyment.

NATHANIEL LEE

To Minne

A picture-frame for you to fill,
    A paltry setting for your face,
A thing that has no worth until
    You lend it something of your grace,

I send (unhappy I that sing
    Laid by awhile upon the shelf)
Because I would not send a thing
    Less charming than you are yourself.

And happier than I, alas!
    (Dumb thing, I envy its delight)
'Twill wish you well, the looking-glass,
    And look you in the face to-night.

ROBERT LOUIS STEVENSON

Lady In The Snow

I saw fair Chloris walk alone,
Whilst feathered rain came softly down,
And Jove descended from his tower
To court her in a silver shower.
The wanton snow flew on her breast
Like little birds unto their nest;
But overcome with whiteness there,
For grief it thawed into a tear;
Thence, falling on her garment's hem,
To deck her, froze into a gem.

WILLIAM STRODE

Lady With A Fan

See how the charming fair
Does break the yielding air,
Which, by her troubled so,
More pure, more smooth, does flow.
Winds without murmurs rise,
Complaining in sad sighs,
Though they dare not repine
How loth they're to resign
Their interest in the fair
To new succeeding air.
How silently they grieve
Their snatched embrace to leave
To new winds, who their place
Supply, and their embrace,
Courting their longer bliss
At every parting kiss,
While with a gentle gale
They swell her painted sail,
Then, trembling, they give way,
Fearing to disobey,

Though fain they her would bear
With every moving air.
In vain, alas, they prove
Unkindness to remove;
In vain to win the field:
Air may, she cannot, yield . . .

RICHARD LEIGH

Epipsychidion

(EXTRACT)

She met me, stranger, upon life's rough way,
And lured me towards sweet death; as night by day,
Winter by spring, or sorrow by swift hope,
Led into light, life, peace. An antelope,
In the suspended impulse of its lightness,
Were less aethereally light: the brightness
Of her divinest presence trembles through
Her limbs, as underneath a cloud of dew
Embodied in the windless heaven of June
Amid the splendour-winged stars, the moon
Burns, inextinguishably beautiful:
And from her lips, as from a hyacinth full
Of honey-dew, a liquid murmur drops,
Killing the sense with passion; sweet as stops
Of planetary music heard in trance.
In her mild lights the starry spirits dance,
The sunbeams of those wells which ever leap
Under the lightnings of the soul – too deep
For the brief fathom-line of thought or sense.
The glory of her being, issuing thence,
Stains the dead, blank, cold air with a warm shade
Of unentangled intermixture, made
By love, of light and motion: one intense
Diffusion, one serene omnipresence,
Whose flowing outlines mingled in their flowing,
Around her cheeks and utmost fingers glowing

With the unintermitted blood, which there
Quivers, (as in a fleece of snow-like air
The crimson pulse of living morning quiver,)
Continuously prolonged, and ending never,
Till they are lost, and in that beauty furled
Which penetrates and clasps and fills the world;
Scarce visible from extreme loveliness.
Warm fragrance seems to fall from her light dress,
And her loose hair; and where some heavy tress
The air of her own speed has disentwined,
The sweetness seems to satiate the faint wind;
And in the soul a wild odour is left,
Beyond the sense, like fiery dews that melt
Into the bosom of a frozen bud. –
See where she stands! a mortal shape indued
With love and life and light and deity,
And motion which may change but cannot die;
An image of some bright eternity;
A shadow of some golden dream; a splendour
Leaving the third sphere pilotless; a tender
Reflection of the eternal moon of love
Under whose motions life's dull billows move;
A metaphor of spring and youth and morning;
A vision like incarnate April, warning,
With smiles and tears, frost the anatomy
Into his summer grave.

PERCY BYSSHE SHELLEY

First Love

I ne'er was struck before that hour,
    With love so sudden and so sweet.
Her face it bloomed like a sweet flower,
    And stole my heart away complete.
My face turned pale a deadly pale,
    My legs refused to walk away,
And when she looked what could I ail,
My life and all seemed turned to clay.

And then my blood rushed to my face,
   And took my eyesight quite away.
The trees and bushes round the place,
   Seemed midnight at noon day.
I could not see a single thing,
   Words from my eyes did start.
They spoke as chords do from the sting,
   And blood burnt round my heart.

Are flowers the winter's choice?
   Is love's bed always snow?
She seemed to hear my silent voice,
   Not love's appeals to know.
I never saw so sweet a face
   As that I stood before.
My heart has left its dwelling place
   And can return no more–.

JOHN CLARE

Song

A scholar first my love implored,
And then an empty titled lord;
The pedant talked in lofty strains;
Alas! his lordship wanted brains:
I listened not, to one or t'other,
But straight referred them to my mother.

A poet next my love assailed,
A lawyer hoped to have prevailed;
The bard too much approved himself,
The lawyer thirsted after pelf:
I listened not, to one or t'other,
Referring still unto my mother.

And after them, some twenty more,
Successless were, as those before;
When Damon, lovely Damon, came!
Our hearts straight felt a mutual flame;
I vowed I'd have him, and no other,
Without referring to my mother.

DOROTHEA DU BOIS

Strephon to Celia.
A Modern Love Letter

Madam

    I hope you'll think it's true
I deeply am in love with you,
When I assure you t'other day,
As I was musing on my way,
At thought of you I tumbled down
Directly in a deadly swoon:
And though 'tis true I'm something better,
Yet I can hardly spell my letter:
And as the latter you may view,
I hope you'll think the former true.
You need not wonder at my flame,
For you are not a mortal dame:
I saw you dropping from the skies;
And let dull idiots swear your eyes
With love their glowing breast inspire,
I tell you they are flames of fire,
That scorch my forehead to a cinder,
And burn my very heart to a tinder.
Your breast so mighty cold, I trow,
Is made of nothing else but snow:
Your hands (no wonder they have charms)
Are made of ivory like your arms.
Your cheeks, that look as if they bled,
Are nothing else but roses red.

Your lips are coral very bright,
Your teeth – though numbers out of spite
May say they're bones – yet 'twill appear
They're rows of pearl exceeding rare.

    Now, madam, as the chat goes round,
I hear you have ten thousand pound:
But that as I a trifle hold,
Give me your person, dem your gold;
Yet for your own sake 'tis secured,
I hope – your houses too insured;
I'd have you take a special care,
And of false mortgages beware;
You've wealth enough 'tis true, but yet
You want a friend to manage it.
Now such a friend you soon might have,
By fixing on your humble slave;
Not that I mind a stately house,
Or value money of a louse;
But your five hundred pounds a year,
I would secure it for my dear:
Then smile upon your slave, that lies
Half murdered by your radiant eyes;
Or else this very moment dies –

Strephon

MARY LEAPOR

A Nosegay For Laura

Come, ye fair, ambrosial flowers,
Leave your beds, and leave your bowers,
Blooming, beautiful, and rare,
Form a posy for my fair;
Fair, and bright, and blooming be,
Meet for such a nymph as she.
Let the young vermilion rose
A becoming blush disclose –

Such as Laura's cheeks display
When she steals my heart away.
Add carnation's varied hue,
Moistened with the morning dew:
To the woodbine's fragrance join
Sprigs of snow-white jessamine.
Add no more: already I
Shall, alas! with envy die,
Thus to see my rival blessed,
Sweetly dying on her breast.

FRANCIS FAWKES

The Gardener's Bonny Daughter

(EXTRACT)

She's sweeter than the first o' spring, more fair than Christmas roses
When robins by the hovel sing, sweet smiles the maid discloses.
Her hair so brown, her eye so bright, as clear as the spring water
I'll go and have a word tonight with the gardener's bonny daughter.

Her cheeks are like the coloured rose, a kiss would surely burn ye.
Her lips are gems more red than those, for love I'll go the journey.
And when the white thorn comes in leaf, and the chaffinch lays
     her lauter
I walk where singing birds are brief w' the gardener's bonny daughter.

I passed the gardener's house one night, my heart burnt to a cinder
When I saw her face and eyes so bright a-looking through the window,
And when I'd passed the house agen, I'd been pounded in a mortar
But she looked and smiled upon me then, so I love the gardener's
     bonny daughter.

JOHN CLARE

Beauty

— A beauty ripe as harvest,
Whose skin is whiter than swan all over,
Than silver, snow, or lilies; a soft lip, that
Would tempt you to eternity of kissing,
And flesh that melteth in the touch to blood,
Bright as your gold, and lovely as your gold,
All her looks are sweet
As the first grapes or cherries.

BEN JONSON

Cherry Ripe

There is a garden in her face
    Where roses and white lilies blow;
A heavenly paradise that place,
    Wherein all pleasant fruits do grow;
There cherries grow that none may buy,
Till 'Cherry-Ripe' themselves do cry.

Those cherries fairly do enclose
    Of orient pearl a double row,
Which when her lovely laughter shows,
    They look like rose-buds fill'd with snow.
Yet them no peer nor prince may buy,
Till 'Cherry-Ripe' themselves do cry.

Her eyes like angels watch them still;
    Her brows like bended bows do stand,
Threat'ning with piercing frowns to kill
    All that approach with eye or hand
These sacred cherries to come nigh,
Till 'Cherry-Ripe' themselves do cry.

THOMAS CAMPION

To A Very Young Lady

Sweetest bud of beauty, may
No untimely frost decay
The early glories, which we trace
Blooming in thy matchless face;
But kindly opening, like the rose,
Fresh beauties every day disclose,
Such as by nature are not shown
In all the blossoms she has blown:
And then, what conquest shall you make,
Who hearts already daily take!
Scorched in the morning with thy beams,
How shall we bear those sad extremes
Which must attend thy threatening eyes
When thou shalt to thy noon arise?

SIR GEORGE ETHEREGE

Thy Perfect Mind

What tho' I'm told that Flora's face
    Is flush'd with fresher tints than thine;
That Chloe moves with nobler grace;
    That Laura's lightnings brighter shine:

What tho' I'm told Zelinda's breast
    Is whiter than the mountain-snows;
That Fulvia's lips, in dimples drest,
    Are sweeter than the summer rose:

For ever hanging on thy smile,
    To others charms my soul is blind:
What perfect form can him beguile?
    Who doats upon thy perfect mind.

FRANK SAYERS

Celia

Not, Celia, that I juster am
    Or better than the rest;
For I would change each hour like them,
    Were not my heart at rest.

But I am tied to very thee
    By every thought I have:
Thy face I only care to see,
    Thy heart I only crave.

All that in woman is adored,
    In thy dear self I find;
For the whole sex can but afford
    The handsome and the kind.

Why then should I seek farther store,
    And still make love anew?
When change itself can give no more,
    'Tis easy to be true.

SIR CHARLES SEDLEY

Amo, Amas, I Love A Lass

Amo, amas,
    I love a lass
As a cedar tall and slender!
    Sweet cowslips' grace
    Is her Nominative Case,
And she's of the Feminine Gender.

Rorum, corum, sunt Divorum!
    Harum scarum Divo!
Tag rag, merry derry, periwig and hatband,
    Hic, hac, horum Genetivo!

Can I decline
A Nymph divine?
Her voice as a flute is *dulcis*!
Her *oculi* bright!
Her *manus* white!
And soft, when I *tacto*, her pulse is!

Rorum, corum, sunt Divorum!
Harum scarum Divo!
Tag rag, merry derry, periwig and hatband,
Hic, hac, horum Genetivo!

O, how *bella*
Is my *Puella*!
I'll kiss *sæculorum*!
If I've luck, Sir!
She's my *Uxor*!
O, dies benedictorum!

Rorum, corum, sunt Divorum!
Harum scarum Divo!
Tag rag, merry derry, periwig and hatband,
Hic, hac, horum Genetivo!

JOHN O'KEEFE

No Loathsomeness In Love

What I fancy, I approve,
No dislike there is in love:
Be my mistress short or tall,
And distorted therewithal:
Be she likewise one of those,
That an acre hath of nose:

Be her forehead, and her eyes
Full of incongruities:
Be her cheeks so shallow too,
As to shew her tongue wag through:
Be her lips ill hung, or set,
And her grinders black as jet;
Has she thin hair, hath she none,
She's to me a paragon.

ROBERT HERRICK

Her Abundance

From DEATH'S JEST BOOK

So fair a creature! of such charms compact
As nature stints elsewhere; which you may find
Under the tender eyelid of a serpent,
Or in the gurge of a kiss-coloured rose,
By drops and sparks: but when she moves, you see,
Like water from a crystal overfilled,
Fresh beauty tremble out of her and lave
Her fair sides to the ground. Of other women,
(And we have beauteous in this court of ours,)
I can remember whether nature touched
Their eye with brown or azure, where a vein
Runs o'er a sleeping eyelid, like some streak
In young blossom; every grace count up,
Here the round turn and crevice of the arm,
There the tress-bunches, or the slender hand
Seen between harpstrings gathering music from them:
But where she is, I'm lost in her abundance
And when she leaves me I know nothing more,
(Like one from whose awakening temples rolls
The cloudy vision of a god away),
Than that she was divine . . .

THOMAS LOVELL BEDDOES

My Mistress' Eyes

My mistress' eyes are nothing like the sun;
Coral is far more red than her lip's red:
If snow be white, why then her breasts are dun;
If hairs be wires, black wires grow on her head.
I have seen roses damasked, red and white,
But no such roses see I in her cheeks;
And in some perfumes is there more delight
Than in the breath that from my mistress reeks.
I love to hear her speak, yet well I know
That music hath a far more pleasing sound;
I grant I never saw a goddess go;
My mistress, when she walks, treads on the ground.
    And yet, by heaven, I think my love as rare
    As any she belied with false compare.

WILLIAM SHAKESPEARE

Upon Julia's Clothes

When as in silks my Julia goes,
Then, then (methinks) how sweetly flows
That liquefaction of her clothes.

Next, when I cast mine eyes and see
That brave vibration each way free;
O how that glittering taketh me!

ROBERT HERRICK

Upon The Nipples Of Julia's Breast

Have ye beheld (with much delight)
A red rose peeping through a white?
Or else a cherry (double graced)
Within a lilies centre placed?
Or ever marked the pretty beam,
A strawberry shewes half-drowned in cream?
Or seen rich rubies blushing through
A pure smooth pearl, and orient too?
So like to this, nay all the rest,
Is each neat niplet of her breast.

ROBERT HERRICK

Love In The Valley

(EXTRACT)

This I may know: her dressing and undressing
    Such a change of light shows as when the skies in sport
Shift from cloud to moonlight; or edging over thunder
    Slips a ray of sun; or sweeping into port
White sails furl; or on the ocean borders
    White sails lean along the waves leaping green.
Visions of her shower before me, but from eyesight
    Guarded she would be like the sun were she seen.

. . . O the golden sheaf, the rustling treasure-armful!
    O the nutbrown tresses nodding interlaced!
O the treasure-tresses one another over
    Nodding! O the girdle slack about the waist!
Slain are the poppies that shot their random scarlet,
    Quick amid the wheatears: wound about the waist,
Gathered, see these brides of earth one blush of ripeness!
    O the nutbrown tresses nodding interlaced!

GEORGE MEREDITH

Delight In Disorder

A sweet disorder in the dress
Kindles in clothes a wantonness:
A lawn about the shoulders thrown
Into a fine distraction:
An erring lace, which here and there
Enthralls the crimson stomacher:
A cuff neglectful, and thereby
Ribbands to flow confusedly:
A winning wave (deserving note)
In the tempestuous petticoat:
A carelesse shoe-string, in whose tie
I see a wild civility:
Do more bewitch me, then when art
Is too precise in every part.

ROBERT HERRICK

Still To Be Neat, Still To Be Drest

Still to be neat, still to be drest,
As you were going to a feast;
Still to be powder'd, still perfumed:
Lady, it's to be presumed,
That arts' hid causes are not found,
All is not sweet, all is not sound.
Give me a look, give me a face;
That makes simplicity a grace;
Robes loosely flowing, hair as free:
Such sweet neglect more taketh me,
Than all th' adulteries of art,
They strike mine eyes, but not my heart.

BEN JONSON

Gloire de Dijon

When she rises in the morning
I linger to watch her;
She spreads the bath-cloth underneath the window
And the sunbeams catch her
Glistening white on the shoulders,
While down her sides the mellow
Golden shadow glows as
She stoops to the sponge, and her swung breasts
Sway like full-blown yellow
Gloire de Dijon roses.

She drips herself with water, and her shoulders
Glisten as silver, they crumple up
Like wet and falling roses, and I listen
For the sluicing of their rain-dishevelled petals.
In the window full of sunlight
Concentrates her golden shadow
Fold on fold, until it glows as
Mellow as the glory roses.

D.H. LAWRENCE

The Magic of Herbs

(EXTRACT)

I asked Philosophy how I should
Have of her the thing I would;
She answered me, when I was able
To make the water malleable;
Or else the way if I could find
To measure out a yard of wind,
Then shalt thou have thine own desire,
When thou canst weigh an ounce of fire.
Unless that thou canst do these three,
Content thyself, thou gett'st not me.

ELIAS ASHMOLE

Two Italian Gentlemen

(EXTRACT)

I serve a mistress whiter than the snow,
    Straighter than cedar, brighter than the glass,
Finer in trip and swifter than the roe,
    More pleasant than the field of flowering grass;
More gladsome to my withering joys that fade
Than winter's sun or summer's cooling shade.
Sweeter than swelling grape of ripest wine,
    Softer than feathers of the fairest swan,
Smoother than jet, more stately than the pine,
    Fresher than poplar, smaller than my span,
Clearer than beauty's fiery-pointed beam,
Or icy crust of crystal's frozen stream.

Yet is she curster than the bear by kind,
    And harder-hearted than the agèd oak,
More glib than oil, more fickle than the wind,
    Stiffer than steel, no sooner bent but broke.
Lo, thus my service is a lasting sore;
Yet will I serve, although I die therefore.

ANTHONY MUNDAY

See Where My Love Sits

Fair is my love that feeds among the lilies,
The lilies growing in that pleasant garden
Where Cupid's mount that well belovèd hill is,
And where that little god himself is warden.
See where my love sits in the beds of spices,
Beset all round with camphor, myrrh, and roses,
And interlaced with curious devices
Which her apart from all the world incloses!
There doth she tune her lute for her delight,
And with sweet music makes the ground to move,
Whilst I, poor I, do sit in heavy plight,
Wailing alone my unrespected love:
    Not daring rush into so rare a place,
    That gives to her, and she to it, a grace.

BARTHOLOMEW GRIFFIN

A Vow To Love Faithfully
Howsoever He Be Rewarded

Set me whereas the sun doth parch the green,
Or where his beams do not dissolve the ice,
In temperate heat, where he is felt, and seen,
In presence pressed of people, mad or wise;
Set me in high, or yet in low degree,
In longest night, or in the shortest day;

In clearest sky, or where clouds thickest be,
In lusty youth, or when my hairs are grey:
Set me in heaven, in earth, or else in hell,
In hill, or dale, or in the foaming flood;
Thrall, or at large, alive whereso I dwell,
Sick, or in health, in evil fame or good;
Hers will I be, and only with this thought,
Content myself, although my chance be nought.

HENRY HOWARD, EARL OF SURREY

A Dialogue Between Cleanthe and Marissa

From THE INQUIRY

Cleanthe Tell me, Marissa, by what rule
May I judge who's the greatest fool?
　　　　*　　　*　　　*
Marissa I'll tell you, since you can't discover:
It is an awkward, whining lover;
Who talks of chains, of flames and passion,
And all the pretty words in fashion;
Words, which are still as true a mark
Of an accomplished modish spark,
As a long wig, or powdered coat:
Like ABC, they're learned by rote;
And then with equal ardour said,
Or to the mistress, or the maid:
An animal for sport design'd,
Both very tame, and very kind:
Who for a smile his soul would give,
And can whole months on glances live:
Who still a slave is to your will,
And whom you with a frown may kill:
Who at your feet whole days will lie,
And watch the motions of your eye:
Will kiss your hand, and fawn, and swear,
That you, and none but you, are fair;

And if he sees that you're inclined
At length his humble suit to mind,
He then all ecstasy will prove,
Is all delight, and joy, and love:
But if you should a look misplace,
Or any favoured rival grace,
He full of rage and of despair,
Nor him, nor you, nor heaven, will spare,
But challenges the happy man,
Who whips him through the lungs; and then
While he is bleeding, begs your pity,
In strains so moving, soft and witty,
That they your heart at length must move
To some remorse, if not to love,
Which he soon guesses by your eyes,
And in an amorous rapture dies.

MARY CHUDLEIGH

A Heart To Love And Grief Inclined

While from our looks, fair nymph, you guess,
   The secret passions of our mind,
My heavy eyes, you say, confess
   A heart to love and grief inclined.

How can I see you, and not love!
   While you, as opening spring, are fair?
While cold as northern blasts you prove,
   How can I love! and not despair?

The wretch in double fetters bound
   Your potent mercy may release:
Soon, if my love by you were crowned,
   Fair prophetess! my grief would cease.

MATTHEW PRIOR

The Enchantment

I did but look and love awhile,
    'Twas but for one half-hour:
Then to resist I had no will,
    And now I have no power.

To sigh and wish is all my ease;
    Sighs which do heat impart
Enough to melt the coldest ice,
    Yet cannot warm your heart.

O would your pity give my heart
    One corner of your breast,
'Twould learn of yours the winning art,
    And quickly steal the rest.

THOMAS OTWAY

The Slight

I did but crave that I might kiss,
    If not her lip, at least her hand,
The coolest lover's frequent bliss;
    And rude is she that will withstand
    That inoffensive liberty:
She (would you think it?) in a fume
Turned her about and left the room;
        Not she, she vowed, not she.

Well, Clarissa, then said I,
    If it must thus for ever be,
I can renounce my slavery
    And, since you will not, can be free.
    Many a time she made me die,
Yet (would you think't!) I loved the more;
But I'll not take't as heretofore,
        Not I, I'll vow, not I.

THOMAS FLATMAN

On Her Pleading Want Of Time

On Thames's bank, a gentle youth
For Lucy sighed with matchless truth –
   Even when he sighed in rhyme.
The lovely maid his flame returned
And would with equal warmth have burned –
   But that she had not time.

Oft he repaired with eager feet
In secret shades his fair to meet
   Beneath the accustomed lime.
She would have fondly met him there
And healed with love each tender care –
   But that she had not time.

'It was not thus, inconstant maid,
You acted once,' the shepherd said,
   'When love was in its prime.'
She grieved to hear him thus complain
And would have writ to ease his pain –
   But that she had not time.

'How can you act so cold part?
No crime of mine has changed your heart –
   If love be not a crime.
We soon must part for months, for years –'
She would have answered with her tears –
   But that she had not time.

GEORGE LYTTELTON

Love In Vain

S. Leave me, simple shepherd, leave me,
    Drag no more a hopeless chain;
   I cannot like, nor would deceive thee:
    Love the maid that loves again.

C. Tho' more gentle nymphs surround me,
        Kindly pitying what I feel,
    Only you have power to wound me,
        Sylvia only you can heal,

S. Corin, cease this idle teasing,
        Love that's forced is harsh and sour;
    If the lover be displeasing,
        To persist, disgusts the more.

C. 'Tis in vain, in vain to fly me,
        Sylvia, I will still pursue;
    Twenty thousand times deny me,
        I will kneel and weep anew.

S. Cupid ne'er shall make me languish,
        I was born averse to love;
    Lover's sighs and tears and anguish,
        Mirth and pastime to me prove.

C. Still I vow with patient duty
        Thus to meet your proudest scorn;
    You for unrelenting Beauty,
        I, for constant love was born.

    But the Fates had not consented,
    Since they both did fickle prove;
    Of her scorn the maid repented;
    And the shepherd of his love.

                              ANNA LETITIA BARBAULD

Love's Philosophy

The fountains mingle with the river
    And the rivers with the ocean,
The winds of heaven mix for ever
    With a sweet emotion;
Nothing in the world is single;
    All things by a law divine
In one spirit meet and mingle.

Why not I with thine? –
See the mountains kiss high heaven
   And the waves clasp one another;
No sister-flower would be forgiven
   If it disdained its brother;
And the sunlight clasps the earth
   And the moonbeams kiss the sea:
What is all this sweet work worth
   If thou kiss not me?

PERCY BYSSHE SHELLEY

The Heart Of Stone

Whence comes my love? O heart, disclose!
It was from cheeks that shame the rose,
From lips that spoil the ruby's praise,
From eyes that mock the diamond's blaze:
Whence comes my woe? as freely own;
Ah me! 'twas from a heart like stone.

The blushing cheek speaks modest mind,
The lips befitting words most kind,
The eye does tempt to love's desire,
And seems to say, ''Tis Cupid's fire';
Yet all so fair but speak my moan,
Since nought doth say the heart of stone

Why thus, my love, so kind bespeak
Sweet eye, sweet lip, sweet blushing cheek, –
Yet not a heart to save my pain?
O Venus, take thy gifts again!
Make not so fair to cause our moan,
Or make a heart that's like your own.

SIR JOHN HARRINGTON

The Lady's Resolve

WRITTEN EXTEMPORE ON A WINDOW

While thirst of praise, and vain desire of fame,
In every age, is every woman's aim;
With courtship pleas'd, of silly toasters proud,
Fond of a train, and happy in a crowd;
On each proud fop bestowing some kind glance,
Each conquest owing to some loose advance;
While vain coquets affect to be pursu'd,
And think they're virtuous, if not grossly lewd:
Let this great maxim be my virtue's guide;
In part she is to blame that has been tried
He comes too near, that comes to be denied.

LADY MARY WORTLEY MONTAGU

What Can I Give Thee Back?

SONNET FROM THE PORTUGUESE VIII

What can I give thee back, O liberal
    And princely giver, who hast brought the gold
    And purple of thine heart, unstained, untold,
And laid them on the outside of the wall
For such as I to take to leave withal,
    In unexpected largesse? Am I cold,
    Ungrateful, that for these most manifold
High gifts, I render nothing back at all?
Not so; not cold, – but very poor instead.
    Ask God who knows. For frequent tears have run
The colours from my life, and left so dead
    And pale a stuff, it were not fitly done
To give the same as pillow to thy head
    Go farther! let it serve to trample on.

ELIZABETH BARRETT BROWNING

No One So Much As You

No one so much as you
Loves this my clay,
Or would lament as you
Its dying day.

You know me through and through
Though I have not told,
And though with what you know
You are not bold.

None ever was so fair
As I thought you:
Not a word can I bear
Spoken against you.

All that I ever did
For you seemed coarse
Compared with what I hid
Nor put in force.

My eyes scarce dare meet you
Lest they should prove
I but respond to you
And do not love.

We look and understand,
We cannot speak
Except in trifles and
Words the most weak.

For I at most accept
Your love, regretting
That is all: I have kept
Only a fretting

That I could not return
All that you gave
And could not ever burn
With the love you have,

Till sometimes it did seem
Better it were
Never to see you more
Than linger here

With only gratitude
Instead of love —
A pine in solitude
Cradling a dove.

EDWARD THOMAS

Mediocrity In Love Rejected

Give me more love, or more disdain;
    The torrid, or the frozen zone
Bring equal ease unto my pain;
    The temperate affords me none:
Either extreme, of love, or hate,
Is sweeter than a calm estate.
Give me a storm; if it be love,
    Like Danaë in that golden shower
I swim in pleasure; if it prove
    Disdain, that torrent will devour
My vulture-hopes; and he's possessed
Of heaven, that's but from hell released:
Then crown my joys, or cure my pain;
Give me more love, or more disdain.

THOMAS CAREW

Song

Strephon hath fashion, wit and youth,
    With all things else that please;
He nothing wants but love and truth
    To ruin me with ease:
But he is flint, and bears the art
    To kindle fierce desire;
His power inflames another's heart,
    Yet he ne'er feels the fire.

O! how it does my soul perplex,
    When I his charms recall,
To think he should despise our sex;
    Or, what's worse, love 'em all!
My wearied heart, like Noah's dove,
    In vain has sought for rest;
Finding no hope to fix my love,
    Returns into my breast.

                      ELIZABETH TAYLOR

I Prythee Send Me Back My Heart

I prythee send me back my heart,
    Since I cannot have thine:
For, if from yours you will not part,
    Why then shouldst thou have mine?

Yet, now I think on't, let it lie;
    To take it were in vain;
For thou'st a thief in either eye
    Would steal it back again.

Why should two hearts in one breast be;
    And yet not lodge together?
Oh love! where is thy sympathy,
    If thus our hearts thou sever?

But love is such a mystery
   I cannot find it out:
For when I think I'm best resolved,
   I then am most in doubt.

Then farewell care! and farewell woe!
   I will no longer pine:
For I'll believe, I have her heart,
   As much as she has mine.

SIR JOHN SUCKLING

The Author's Resolution In A Sonnet

Shall I wasting in despair
Die because a woman's fair?
Or make pale my cheeks with care
'Cause another's rosy are?
Be she fairer than the day,
Or the flowery meads in May,
   If she think not well of me,
   What care I how fair she be?

Shall my silly heart be pined
'Cause I see a woman kind?
Or a well-disposed nature
Joined with a lovely feature?
Be she meeker, kinder than
Turtle-dove or pelican,
   If she be not so to me
   What care I how kind she be?

Shall a woman's virtues move
Me to perish for her love?
Or her well-deservings known
Make me quite forget mine own?
Be she with that goodness blest
Which may merit name of best,
   If she be not such to me
   What care I how good she be?

'Cause her fortune seems too high,
Shall I play the fool and die?
She that bears a noble mind,
If not outward helps she find,
Thinks what with them he would do
That without them dares her woo;
    And unless that mind I see
    What care I how great she be?

Great, or good, or kind, or fair,
I will ne'er the more despair;
If she love me, this believe,
I will die, ere she shall grieve:
If she slight me when I woo
I can scorn and let her go,
    For if she be not for me
    What care I for whom she be.

GEORGE WITHER

The Resolute Courtier

Prithee, say aye or no;
If thou'lt not have me, tell me so;
    I cannot stay,
    Nor will I wait upon
      A smile or frown.
If thou wilt have me, say;
Then I am thine, or else I am mine own.

Be white or black; I hate
Dependence on a checkered fate;
    Let go, or hold;
    Come, either kiss or not:
      Now to be hot,
    And then again as cold,
Is a fantastic fever you have got.

A tedious woo is base,
And worse by far than a long grace:
For whilst we stay,
Our lingering spoils the roast,
Or stomach's lost;
Nor can, nor will I stay;
For if I sup not quickly, I will fast.

Whilst we are fresh and stout
And vigorous, let us to 't:
Alas, what good
From wrinkled man appears,
Gelded with years,
When his thin wheyish blood
Is far less comfortable than his tears?

THOMAS SHIPMAN

If You Love Me, Don't Pursue Me

Get you gone, you will undo me!
If you love me, don't pursue me;
Let that inclination perish
Which I dare no longer cherish;
At ev'ry hour, in ev'ry place,
I either see or form your face;
My dreams at night are all of you!
Such as 'til now I never knew:
I've sported thus with young-desire,
Never intending to go higher.
You found me harmless; leave me so;
For were I not – you'd leave me too.

SIR CHARLES SEDLEY

Love That Never Told Can Be

Never seek to tell thy love,
    Love that never told can be;
For the gentle wind doth move
    Silently, invisibly.

I told my love, I told my love,
    I told her all my heart;
Trembling, cold, in ghastly fears.
    Ah! she did depart!

Soon after she was gone from me,
    A traveller came by,
Silently, invisibly:
    He took her with a sigh.

WILLIAM BLAKE

A Petition

Lady, whom my belovèd loves so well!
    When on his clasping arm thy head reclineth,
When on thy lips his ardent kisses dwell,
    And the bright flood of burning light that shineth
In his dark eyes, is pourèd into thine;
    When thou shalt lie enfolded to his heart
    In all the trusting helplessness of love;
    If in such joy sorrow can find a part,
Oh, give one sigh unto a doom like mine!
    Which I would have thee pity, but not prove.
One cold, calm, careless, wintry look that fell
    Haply by chance on one, is all that he
Ever gave my love; round that, my wild thoughts dwell
    In one eternal pang of memory.

FANNY KEMBLE

The Divorce

Dear, back my wounded heart restore,
    And turn away thy powerful eyes;
Flatter my willing soul no more!
    Love must not hope what fate denies.

Take, take away thy smiles and kisses!
    Thy love wounds deeper than disdain,
For he that sees the heaven he misses
    Sustains two hells, of loss and pain . . .

THOMAS STANLEY

To J.G. On The News Of His Marriage

My love? alas! I must not call you mine,
But to your envied bride that name resign:
I must forget your lovely melting charms,
And be for ever banished from your arms:
For ever? oh! the horror of that sound!
It gives my bleeding heart a deadly wound:
While I might hope, although my hope was vain,
It gave some ease to my unpitied pain,
But now your marriage doth all hope exclude,
And but to think is sin; yet you intrude
On every thought; if I but close my eyes,
Methinks your pleasing form beside me lies;
With every sigh I gently breathe your name,
Yet no ill thoughts pollute my hallowed flame;
'Tis pure and harmless, as a lambent fire,
And never mingled with a warm desire:
All I have now to ask of bounteous heaven,
Is, that your perjuries may be forgiven:
That she who you have with your nuptials blest,
As she's the happiest wife, may prove the best:
That all our joys may light on you alone,
Then I can be contented to have none:

And never wish that you should kinder be,
Than now and then, to cast a thought on me:
And, madam, though the conquest you have won
Over my Strephon, has my hopes undone;
I'll daily beg of heaven, he may be
Kinder to you, than he has been to me.

'EPHELIA'

To My Rival

Since you dare brave me, with a rival's name,
You shall prevail, and I will quit my claim:
For know, proud maid, I scorn to call him mine,
Whom thou durst ever hope to have made thine:
Yet I confess, I loved him once so well,
His presence was my heaven, his absence hell:
With gen'rous excellence I filled his breast,
And in sweet beauteous forms his person dressed;
For him I did heaven and its power despise,
And only lived by th'influence of his eyes:
I feared not rivals, for I thought that he
That was possessed of such a prize as me,
All meaner objects would contemn, and slight,
Nor let an abject thing usurp my right:
But when I heard he was so wretched base
To pay devotion to thy wrinkled face
I banished him my sight, and told the slave,
He had not worth, but what my fancy gave:
'Twas I that raised him to this glorious state,
And can as easily annihilate:
But let him live, branded with guilt and shame,
And shrink into the shade from whence he came;
His punishment shall be the loss of me,
And be augmented by his gaining thee.

'EPHELIA'

The Lord Of The Isles

(EXTRACT)

No! sum thine Edith's wretched lot
In these brief words. He loves her not.

SIR WALTER SCOTT

The Maid Of Neidpath

O lovers' eyes are sharp to see,
    And lovers' ears in hearing;
And love, in life's extremity,
    Can lend an hour of cheering.
Disease had been in Mary's bower,
    And slow decay from mourning.
Though now she sits on Neidpath's Tower,
    To watch her love's returning.

All sunk and dim her eyes so bright,
    Her form decayed by pining,
Till through her wasted hand, at night,
    You saw the taper shining;
By fits, a sultry hectic hue
    Across her cheek was flying;
By fits, so ashy pale she grew,
    Her maidens thought her dying.

Yet keenest powers to see and hear
    Seemed in her frame residing;
Before the watch-dog prick'd his ear
    She heard her lover's riding;
Ere scarce a distant form was ken'd,
    She knew, and waved to greet him;
And o'er the battlement did bend,
    As on the wing to meet him.

He came – he passed – an heedless gaze,
    As o'er some stranger glancing;
Her welcome, spoke in faltering phrase,
    Lost in his courser's prancing.
The castle arch, whose hollow tone
    Returns each whisper spoken,
Could scarcely catch the feeble moan
    Which told her heart was broken.

SIR WALTER SCOTT

How Lisa Loved The King

(EXTRACT)

. . . She watched all day that she might see him pass
With knights and ladies; but she said, 'Alas!
Though he should see me, it were all as one
He saw a pigeon sitting on the stone
Of wall or balcony: some coloured spot
His eye just sees, his mind regardeth not.
I have no music-touch that could bring nigh
My love to his soul's hearing. I shall die,
And he will never know who Lisa was –
The trader's child, whose soaring spirit rose
As hedge-born aloe flowers that rarest years disclose . . .'

GEORGE ELIOT

Chop-Cherry

Thou gav'st me leave to kiss,
    Thou gav'st me leave to woo;
Thou mad'st me think, by this
    And that, thou lov'st me too.

But I shall ne'er forget
    How, for to make thee merry
Thou mad'st me chop, but yet
    Another snapped the cherry.

ROBERT HERRICK

The Vain-Love

(EXTRACT)

. . . I sought not from thee a return,
But without hopes or fears did burn;
My covetous passion did approve
The hoarding up, not use, of love.
My love a kind of dream was grown,
A foolish, but a pleasant one;
From which I'm wakened now, but, oh!
Prisoners to die are weakened so:
For now the effects of loving are
Nothing but longings with despair:
Despair, whose torments no men, sure,
But lovers, and the damned endure . . .

ABRAHAM COWLEY

Renouncement

I must not think of thee; and, tired yet strong,
I shun the thought that lurks in all delight –
The thought of thee – and in the blue heaven's height,
And in the sweetest passage of a song.
O just beyond the fairest thoughts that throng
This breast, the thought of thee waits, hidden yet bright;
But it must never, never come in sight;
I must stop short of thee the whole day long.

But when sleep comes to close each difficult day,
When night gives pause to the long watch I keep,
And all my bonds I needs must loose apart,
And doff my will as raiment laid away, –
With the first dream that comes with the first sleep,
I run, I run, I am gathered to thy heart.

ALICE MEYNELL

And On My Eyes Dark Sleep By Night

Come, dark-eyed sleep, thou child of night,
Give me thy dreams, thy lies;
Lead through the horny portal white
The pleasure day denies.

O bring the kiss I could not take
From lips that would not give;
Bring me the heart I could not break,
The bliss for which I live.

I care not if I slumber blest
By fond delusion; nay,
Put me on Phaon's lips to rest,
And cheat the cruel day!

MICHAEL FIELD

Sometimes With One I Love

Sometimes with one I love I fill myself with rage for fear I effuse
    unreturn'd love,
But now I think there is no unreturn'd love, the pay is certain
    one way or another,
(I loved a certain person ardently and my love was not return'd,
Yet out of that I have written these songs.)

WALT WHITMAN

PERSUASION & DISHONOUR

A Coy Heart

O what pleasure 'tis to find
    A coy heart melt by slow degrees!
When to yielding 'tis inclined,
    Yet her fear a ruin sees;
When her tears do kindly flow
And her sighs do come and go.

O how charming 'tis to meet
    Soft resistance from the fair,
When her pride and wishes meet
    And by turns increase her care;
O how charming 'tis to know
She would yield but can't tell how!

O how pretty is her scorn
    When, confused 'twixt love and shame,
Still refusing, tho' she burn,
    The soft pressures of my flame!
Her pride in her denial lies
And mine is in my victories.

APHRA BEHN

Pursuit

King Edward.
Thou hear'st me say that I do dote on thee.

Countess of Salisbury.
If on my beauty, take it if thou canst;
Though little, I do prize it ten times less;
If on my virtue, take it if thou canst;
For virtue's store by giving doth augment.

Be it on what it will, that I can give,
And thou canst take away, inherit it.

King
It is thy beauty I would enjoy.

Countess
O were it painted, I would wipe it off,
And dispossess myself to give it thee;
But, sovereign, it is soldered to my life:
Take one, and both; for, like an humble shadow,
It haunts the sunshine of my summer's life.

King
But thou may'st lend it me to sport withal.

Countess
As easy may my intellectual soul
Be lent away, and yet my body live,
As lend my body (palace to my soul)
Away from her, and yet retain my soul.
My body is her bower, her court, her abbey,
And she an angel, pure, divine, unspotted;
If I should lend her house, my lord, to thee,
I kill my poor soul, and my poor soul me . . .

ANONYMOUS

The Repulse To Alcander

(EXTRACT)

Yet know, base man, I scorn your lewd amours,
Hate them from all, not only 'cause they're yours.
Oh sacred love! let not the world profane
Thy transports, thus to sport and entertain;
The beau, with some small artifice of's own,
Can make a treat for all the wanton town.
I thought myself secure within these shades,
But your rude love my privacy invades,
Affronts my virtue, hazards my just fame:

Why should I suffer for your lawless flame?
For oft 'tis known, through vanity and pride,
Men boast those favours which they are denied;
Or others' malice, which can soon discern,
Perhaps may see in you some kind concern,
So scatter false suggestions of their own,
That I love too: oh, stain to my renown!
No, I'll be wise, avoid your sight in time,
And shun at once the censure and the crime.

SARAH EGERTON

Honour

She loves, and she confesses too;
There's then at last no more to do.
The happy work's entirely done;
Enter the town which thou has won;
The fruits of conquest now begin;
Iô triumph! Enter in.

What's this, ye Gods, what can it be?
Remains there still an enemy?
Bold honour stands up in the gate,
And would yet capitulate;
Have I o'ercome all real foes,
And shall this phantom me oppose?

Noisy nothing! stalking shade!
By what witchcraft wert thou made?
Empty cause of solid harms!
But I shall find out counter charms
Thy airy devilship to remove
From this circle here of love.

Sure I shall rid myself of thee
By the night's obscurity,
And obscure secrecy.
Unlike to every other spright,
Thou attempt'st not men t'affright,
Nor appear'st but in the light.

ABRAHAM COWLEY

Song

Ye virgin powers! defend my heart
　　From amorous looks and smiles;
From saucy love, or nicer art
　　Which most our sex beguiles.

From sighs, from vows, from awful fears
　　That do to pity move;
From speaking-silence, and from tears,
　　Those springs that water love.

But, if thro' passion I grow blind,
　　Let honour be my guide;
And where frail nature seems inclined,
　　There place a guard of pride.

A heart whose flames are seen, tho' pure,
　　Needs every virtue's aid;
And those who think themselves secure,
　　The soonest are betrayed.

ELIZABETH TAYLOR

Phyllis

Poor credulous and simple maid!
By what strange wiles art thou betrayed!
A treasure thou has lost today
For which thou can'st no ransom pay.
How black art thou transformed with sin!
How strange a guilt gnaws me within!
Grief will convert this red to pale;
When every wake, and witsund-ale
Shall talk my shame; break, break sad heart
There is no medecine for my smart,
    No herb nor balm can cure my sorrow,
    Unless you meet again tomorrow.

THOMAS RANDOLPH

A Song

What torments must the virgin prove
    That feels the pangs of hopeless love.
What endless cares must rack the breast
    That is by sure despair possessed.

When love in tender bosoms reigns,
    With all its soft, its pleasing pains,
Why should it be a crime to own
    The fatal flame we cannot shun?

The soul by nature formed sincere
    A slavish forced disguise must wear,
Lest the unthinking world reprove
    The heart that glows with generous love.

But oh! in vain the sigh's repressed,
    That gently heaves the pensive breast,
The glowing blush, the falling tear,
    The conscious wish, and silent fear.

Ye soft betrayers, aid my flame,
    And give my new desires a name;
Some power my gentle griefs redress,
    Reveal, or make my passion less.

CHARLOTTE LENNOX

Dialogue After Enjoyment

She   What have we done? what cruel passion moved thee,
        Thus to ruin her that loved thee?
    Me thou has robbed, but what art thou
    Thyself the richer now?
        Shame succeeds the short-lived pleasure;
    So soon is spent, and gone, this thy ill-gotten treasure.

He   We have done no harm; nor was it theft to me,
        But noblest charity in thee.
    I'll the well-gotten pleasure
    Safe in my memory treasure;
        What though the flower itself do waste,
    The essence from it drawn does long and sweeter last.

She   No: I'm undone; my honour thou hast slain,
        And nothing can restore't again.
    Art and labour to bestow,
    Upon the carcase of it now,
        Is but t'embalm a body dead,
    The figure may remain, the life and beauty's fled.

He   Never, my dear, was honour yet undone
        By love, but indiscretion.
    To the wise it all things does allow;
    And cares not what we do; but how.
        Like tapers shut in ancient urns,
    Unless it let in air, forever shines and burns.

She   Thou first perhaps who did'st the fault commit,
        Wilt make thy wicked boast of it.
    For men, with Roman pride, above
    The conquest, do the triumph love:
        Nor think a perfect victory gained,
    Unless they through the streets their captive lead enchained.

He   Whoe'er his secret joys has open laid,
        The baud to his own wife is made.
    Beside what boast is left for me,
    Whose whole wealth's a gift from thee?
        'Tis you the conqueror are, 'tis you
    Who have not only ta'en, but bound and gagged me too.

She   Though public punishment we escape, the sin
        Will rack and torture us within:
    Guilt and sin our bosom bears;
    And though fair, yet the fruit appears,
        That worm which now the core does waste
    When long't has gnawed within will break the skin at last.

He   That thirsty drink, that hungry food I sought,
        That wounded balm, is all my fault.
    And thou in pity didst apply,
    The kind and only remedy:
        The cause absolves the crime; since me
    So mighty force did move, so mighty goodness thee.

She   Curse on thine arts! methinks I hate thee now;
        And yet I'm sure I love thee too!
    I'm angry, but my wrath will prove,
    More innocent than did thy love.
        Thou hast this day undone me quite;
    Yet wilt undo me more should'st thou not come at night.

ABRAHAM COWLEY

Chloris

Chloris, I cannot say your eyes
Did my unwary heart surprise;
Nor will I swear it was your face,
Your shape, or any nameless grace;
For, you are so entirely fair,
To love a part injustice were:
No drowning man can know which drop
Of water his last breath did stop:
So when the stars in heaven appear,
And join to make the night look clear,
The light we no one's bounty call,
But the obliging gift of all.
He that does lips or hand adore,
Deserves them only and no more;
But I love all and every part,
And nothing less can ease my heart . . .

SIR CHARLES SEDLEY

To His Coy Mistress

Had we but world enough, and time,
This coyness, Lady, were no crime.
We would sit down, and think which way
To walk, and pass our long love's day.
Thou by the Indian Ganges side
Should'st rubies find: I by the tide
Of Humber would complain. I would
Love you ten years before the Flood:
And you should if you please refuse
Till the conversion of the Jews.
My vegetable love should grow
Vaster than empires, and more slow.
An hundred years should go to praise
Thine eyes, and on thy forehead gaze.

Two hundred to adore each breast:
But thirty thousand to the rest.
An age at least to every part,
And the last age should show your heart.
For, Lady, you deserve this state;
Nor would I love at lower rate.

    But at my back I always hear
Time's wingèd chariot drawing near:
And yonder all before us lie
Deserts of vast eternity.
Thy beauty shall no more be found;
Nor, in thy marble vault, shall sound
My echoing song: then worms shall try
That long preserved virginity:
And your quaint honour turn to dust;
And into ashes all my lust.
The grave's a fine and private place,
But none I think do there embrace.

    Now therefore, while the youthful hue
Sits on thy skin like morning dew,
And while thy willing soul transpires
At every pore with instant fires,
Now let us sport us while we may;
And now, like amorous birds of prey,
Rather at once our time devour,
Than languish in his slow-chapt power.
Let us roll all our strength, and all
Our sweetness, up into one ball:
And tear our pleasures with rough strife,
Thorough the iron gates of life.
Thus, though we cannot make our sun
Stand still, yet we will make him run.

ANDREW MARVELL

Trust Not Those Curlèd Waves of Gold

Trust not, sweet soul, those curlèd waves of gold
With gentle tides which on your temples flow,
Nor temples spread with flecks of virgin snow,
Nor snow of cheeks with Tyrian grain enrolled.
Trust not those shining lights which wrought my woe,
When first I did their burning rays behold,
Nor voice, whose sounds more strange effects do show
Than of the Thracian Harper have been told:
Look to this dying lily, fading rose,
Dark hyacinth, of late whose blushing beams
Made all the neighbouring herbs and grass rejoice,
And think how little is twixt life's extremes:
    The cruel tyrant that did kill those flow'rs,
    Shall once (aye me!) not spare that spring of yours.

WILLIAM DRUMMOND

Go, Lovely Rose

    Go, lovely rose –
Tell her that wastes her time and me,
    That now she knows,
When I resemble her to thee,
How sweet and fair she seems to be.

    Tell her that's young
And shuns to have her graces spied,
    That hadst thou sprung
In deserts where no men abide,
Thou must have uncommended died.

    Small is the worth
Of beauty from the light retired:
    Bid her come forth,
Suffer herself to be desired,
And not blush so to be admired.

> Then die! – that she
> The common fate of all things rare
>   May read in thee;
> How small a part of time they share
> That are so wondrous sweet and fair!

EDMUND WALLER

Beauty, Time and Love

(EXTRACT)

When men shall find thy flower, thy glory, pass,
And thou with careful brow, sitting alone,
Receivèd hast this message from thy glass,
That tells the truth and says that all is gone;
Fresh shalt thou see in me the wounds thou mad'st:
Though spent thy flame, in me the heat remaining:
I that have loved thee thus before thou fad'st –
My faith shall wax, when thou are in thy waning.
The world shall find this miracle in me,
That fire can burn when all the matter's spent:
Then what my faith hath been thyself shall see,
And that thou was unkind thou may'st repent. –
    Thou may'st repent that thou has scorned my tears,
    When winter snows upon thy sable hairs.

SAMUEL DANIEL

The Amorous War

(EXTRACT)

> Time is a feathered thing,
>   And, whilst I praise
> The sparklings of thy looks and call them rays,
>   Takes wing,
>   Leaving behind him as he flies

An unperceivèd dimness in thine eyes.
  His minutes, whilst they're told,
    Do make us old;
  And every sand of his fleet glass,
  Increasing age as it doth pass,
  Insensibly sows wrinkles there
  Where flowers and roses do appear.
  Whilst we do speak, our fire
  Doth into ice expire,
    Flames turn to frost;
    And ere we can
  Know how our crow turns swan,
  Or how a silver snow
  Springs there where jet did grow,
Our fading spring is in dull winter lost.

Since, then, the night hath hurled
    Darkness, love's shade,
  Over its enemy the day, and made
    The world
  Just such a blind and shapeless thing
As 'twas before light did from darkness spring,
  Let us employ its treasure
  And make shade pleasure:
Let's number out the hours by blisses,
And count the minutes by our kisses;
  Let the heavens new motions feel
  And by our embraces wheel;
  And, whilst we try the way
  By which Love doth convey
    Soul unto soul,
    And mingling so
  Makes them such raptures know
  As makes them entrancèd lie
    In mutual ectasy,
Let the harmonious spheres in music roll!

JASPER MAYNE

Faerie Queene

(EXTRACT)

So passeth in the passing of a day,
Of mortal life the leaf, the bud, the flower;
No more doth flourish after first decay
That erst was sought to deck both bed and bower
Of many a lady, and many a paramour.
Gather therefore the rose whilst yet is prime,
For soon comes age that will her pride deflower;
Gather the rose of love whilest yet is time,
Whilst loving thou mayst loved be with equal crime.

EDMUND SPENSER

To The Virgins

Gather ye rosebuds while ye may,
    Old Time is still a-flying;
And this same flower that smiles to day,
    To-morrow will be dying.

The glorious lamp of heaven, the sun,
    The higher he's a-getting,
The sooner will his race be run,
    And nearer he's to setting.

That age is best which is the first,
    When youth and blood are warmer;
But being spent, the worse and worst
    Times still succeed the former.

Then be not coy, but use your time,
    And while ye may, go marry:
For having lost but once your prime,
    You may for ever tarry.

ROBERT HERRICK

To Delia

Look Delia, how w'esteem the half-blown rose,
The image of thy blush, and summer's honour!
Whilst yet her tender bud doth undisclose
That full of beauty time bestows upon her:
No sooner spreads her glory in the air,
But strait her wide-blown pomp comes to decline;
She then is scorned, that late adorned the fair;
So fade the roses of those cheeks of thine!
No April can revive thy withered flowers,
Whose springing grace adorns thy glory now:
Swift speedy time, feathered with flying hours,
Dissolves the beauty of the fairest brow,
  Then do not thou such treasure waste in vain
  But love now, whilst thou may'st be loved again.

SAMUEL DANIEL

Love In Thy Youth, Fair Maid

Love in thy youth, fair maid; be wise,
  Old time will make thee colder,
And though each morning new arise
  Yet we each day grow older.

Thou as heaven art fair and young,
  Thine eyes like twin stars are shining:
But ere another day be sprung,
  All these will be declining.

Then winter comes with all his fears
  And all thy sweets shall borrow;
Too late then wilt thou shower thy tears,
  And I too late shall sorrow.

ANONYMOUS

To A.L. Persuasions To Love

Starve not yourself, because you may
Thereby make me pine away;
Nor let brittle beauty make
You your wiser thoughts forsake:
For that lovely face will fail,
Beauty's sweet, but beauty's frail;
'Tis sooner past, 'tis sooner done
Than summer's rain, or winter's sun;
Most fleeting when it is most dear,
'Tis gone white we but say 'tis here.
These curious locks so aptly twined,
Whose every hair a soul doth bind,
Will change their auburn hue, and grow
White, and cold as winter's snow.
That eye which now is Cupid's nest
Will prove his grave, and all the rest
Will follow; in the cheek, chin, nose,
Nor lily shall be found nor rose.
And what will then become of all
Those, whom now you servants call?
Like swallows when their summer's done,
They'll fly and seek some warmer sun.

THOMAS CAREW

Sonnet 26

I'll give thee leave, my love, in beauty's field
To rear red colours whiles, and bend thine eyes;
Those that are bashful still, I quite despise
Such simple souls are too soon moved to yield:
Let majesty armed in thy count'nance sit,
As that which will no injury receive;
And I'll not hate thee, whiles although thou have
A spark of pride, so it be ruled by wit.

This is to chastity a powerful guard,
Whilst haughty thoughts all servile things eschew,
That spark hath power the passions to subdue,
And would of glory challenge a reward:
　　　But do not fall in love with thine own self;
　　　Narcissus erst was lost on such a shelf.

SIR WILLIAM ALEXANDER, EARL OF STIRLING

Hapless Beauty!

Such is the fatal growth of hapless beauty!
In her soft spring she puts forth tender buds
And blooming flowers, which the sun's genial warmth
Calls forth to fruit, and ripens to high taste:
When comes the savage, the despoiler, man
With hand rapacious ravages the boughs,
And leaves her naked, stripped of all her honours.

PHILIP FROWDE

The Caution

Soft kisses may be innocent;
But ah! too easy maid, beware;
Tho' that is all thy kindness meant,
'Tis love's delusive, fatal snare.

No virgin e'er at first design'd
Thro' all the maze of love to stray;
But each new path allures her mind,
Till wandering on, she lose her way.

'Tis easy ere set out to stay;
But who the useful art can teach,
When sliding down a steepy way,
To stop, before the end we reach?

Keep ever something in thy power,
Beyond what would thy honour stain:
He will not dare to aim at more,
Who for small favours sighs in vain.

CATHERINE COCKBURN

A Maid's Lament

Ah, false Amyntas, can that hour
    So soon forgotten be
When first I yielded up my power
    To be betrayed by thee?
God knows with how much innocence
    I did my heart resign,
Unto thy faithless eloquence,
    And gave thee what was mine.

I had not one reserve in store,
    But at thy feet I laid
Those arms which conquered heretofore,
    Tho' now thy trophies made,
Thy eyes in silence told their tale,
    Of love in such a way,
That 'twas as easy to prevail,
    As after to betray.

APHRA BEHN

Ballad

A faithless shepherd courted me,
He stole away my liberty;
When my poor heart was strange to men
He came and smiled and stole it then.

When my apron would hang low
Me he sought through frost and snow;
When it puckered up with shame
And I sought him, he never came.

When summer brought no fears to fright,
He came to guard me every night;
When winter nights did darkly prove,
None came to guard me or to love.

I wish, I wish – but it's in vain –
I wish I was a maid again;
A maid again I cannot be:
O when will green grass cover me?

I wish my babe had ne'er been born;
I've made its pillow on a thorn.
I wish my sorrows all away,
My soul with God, my body clay.

He promised beds as fine as silk
And sheets for love as white as milk
But he when won my heart astray
Left me to want a bed of clay.

He kept his sheep on yonder hill,
His heart seemed soft but it was steel;
I ran with love and was undone,
O had I walked ere I did run.

He has two hearts and I have none;
He'll be a rogue, when I am gone,
To thee, my baby, unto thee,
As he has been too long to me.

I weep the past, I dread the gloom
Of sorrows in the time to come;
When thou without a friend shalt be
Weeping on a stranger's knee.

My heart would break – but it is brass –
To see thee smile upon my face,
To see thee smile at words that be
The messengers of grief to thee.

I wish, my child, thou'dst ne'er been born,
I've made thy pillow on a thorn;
I wish our sorrows both away,
Our souls with God, our bodies clay.

ANONYMOUS

To A Lady Making Love

Good madam, when ladies are willing,
    A man must needs look like a fool;
For me I would not give a shilling
    For one who would love out of rule.

You should leave us to guess by your blushing,
    And not speak the matter so plain;
'Tis ours to write and be pushing,
    'Tis yours to affect disdain.

That you're in a terrible taking,
    By all these sweet oglings I see,
But the fruit that can fall without shaking,
    Indeed is too mellow for me.

LADY MARY WORTLEY MONTAGU

Song

When lovely woman stoops to folly,
    And finds too late that men betray,
What charm can sooth her melancholy,
    What art can wash her guilt away?

The only art her guilt to cover,
    To hide her shame from every eye,
To give repentance to her lover,
    And wring his bosom – is to die.

OLIVER GOLDSMITH

The Honour Of A Maid

From ALL'S WELL THAT ENDS WELL

The honour of a maid is her name,
And no legacy is so rich as honesty;
Beware, Diana, of gallants; their promises, enticements,
Oaths, tokens, and all those engines of a lust,
Are not the things they go under: many a maid
Hath been seduced by them; and the misery is, example,
That so terribly shows the wreck of maidenhood,
Cannot, for all that, dissuade succession; but that
They are lined with the twigs that threaten them.
I hope I need not advise you further. But I hope
Your own grace will keep you where you are;
Tho' there were no farther danger known,
But the modesty which is so lost.

WILLIAM SHAKESPEARE

Angellica's Lament

Had I remained in innocent security,
I should have thought all men were born my slaves,
And worn my power like lightning in my eyes,
To have destroyed at pleasure when offended.
– But when love held the mirror, the undeceiving glass
Reflected all the weakness of my soul, and made me know
My richest treasure being lost, my honour,
All the remaining spoil could not be worth
The conqueror's care or value.
– Oh how I fell like a long-worshipped idol
Discovering all the cheat.

APHRA BEHN

KISSING

First Time He Kissed Me

SONNET FROM THE PORTUGUESE XXXVIII

First time he kissed me; he but only kissed
The fingers of this hand wherewith I write,
And ever since it grew more clean and white, . .
Slow to world-greetings . . quick with its 'Oh, list,'
When the angels speak. A ring of amethyst
I could not wear here plainer to my sight,
Than that first kiss. The second passed in height
The first, and sought the forehead, and half missed,
Half falling on the hair. O beyond meed!
That was the chrism of love, which love's own crown,
With sanctifying sweetness, did precede.
The third, upon my lips, was folded down
In perfect, purple state! since when, indeed,
I have been proud and said, "My Love, my own."

ELIZABETH BARRETT BROWNING

Love On Ice

The last rose-petal of the sunset's rose
Falls in the further west and faintly glows,
One thought of fire in a world of snows.

She turns, I turn with her. The level rays
Of the low moon half veiled in opal haze
With rose-white magic light the eastward ways.

She flies, I follow. Through the glimmering plain
We speed in silence. When I strive to gain
Her side, she holds me back. Wild hopes and vain!

She flies, I follow. Thus her power I own
That am her poor, obsequious shadow grown –
For still I touch her, still I'm left alone!

She flies, I follow. Though her finger-tips
Are all I hold, yet at her unseen lips
My soul flits on before, and bee-like sips.

She flies, I follow. Hear the dulcet chime
Of steel on ice that marks the magic time,
And breaks the rhythmic silence as with rhyme!

She trips, she falls. I hold her in a trice
And colder were her lips than northern ice,
But warmer was my kiss than southern skies.

                                        E.B. OSBORN

In A Gondola

The moth's kiss, first!
Kiss me as if you made believe
You were not sure, this eve,
How my face, your flower, had pursed
Its petals up; so, here and there
You brush it, till I grow aware
Who wants me, and wide ope I burst.

The bee's kiss, now!
Kiss me as if you entered gay
My heart at some noonday,
A bud that dares not disallow
The claim, so all is rendered up,
And passively its shattered cup
Over your head to sleep I bow.

                              ROBERT BROWNING

Take, Oh Take Those Lips Away

Take, oh take those lips away,
    That so sweetly were forsworn,
And those eyes, the break of day,
    Lights that do mislead the morn.
But my kisses bring again,
Seals of love, but sealed in vain.

Hide, oh hide those hills of snow,
    Which thy frozen bosom bears,
On whose tops the pinks that grow
    Are yet of those that April wears.
But first set my poor heart free,
Bound in those icy chains by thee.

JOHN FLETCHER

Give Me A Kiss

Give me a kiss from those sweet lips of thine
And make it double by enjoining mine,
Another yet, nay yet and yet another,
And let the first kiss be the second's brother.
Give me a thousand kisses and yet more;
And then repeat those that have gone before;
Let us begin while daylight springs in heaven,
And kiss till night descends into the even,
And when that modest secretary, night,
Discolours all but thy heaven beaming bright,
We will begin revels of hidden love
In that sweet orb where silent pleasures move.
In high new strains, unspeakable delight,
We'll vent the dull hours of the silent night:
Were the bright day no more to visit us,
Oh, then for ever would I hold thee thus,
Naked, enchained, empty of idle fear,
As the first lovers in the garden were.

I'll die betwixt thy breasts that are so white,
For, to die there, would do a man delight.
Embrace me still, for time runs on before,
And being dead we shall embrace no more.
Let us kiss faster than the hours do fly,
Long live each kiss and never know to die . . .
Let us vie kisses, till our eyelids cover,
And if I sleep, count me an idle lover;
Admit I sleep, I'll still pursue the theme,
And eagerly I'll kiss thee in a dream . . .

ANONYMOUS

The Forest

(EXTRACT)

Kiss me, sweet: the wary lover
Can your favours keep, and cover,
When the common courting jay
All your bounties will betray.
Kiss again: no creature comes.
Kiss, and score up wealthy sums
On my lips, thus hardly sundered
While you breathe. First give a hundred.
Then a thousand, then another
Hundred, then unto the other
Add a thousand, and so more:
Till you equal with the store,
All the grass that Rumney yields,
Or the sands in Chelsea fields,
Or the drops in silver Thames,
Or the stars that gild his streams,
In the silent summer-nights,
When youths ply their stol'n delights . . .

BEN JONSON

The Honey And The Bee

To heal the wound a bee had made
  Upon my Kitty's face,
Honey upon her cheek she laid,
  And bid me kiss the place.

Please, I obeyed, and from the wound
  Imbibed both sweet and smart,
The honey on my lips I found,
  The sting within my heart.

                                                 ANONYMOUS

Stealing A Kiss

Alas! madam, for stealing of a kiss,
  Have I so much your mind then offended?
Have I then done so grievously amiss,
  That by no means it may be amended?
Then revenge you, and the next way is this.
  Another kiss shall have my life ended.
For to my mouth the first my heart did suck,
The next shall clean out of my breast it pluck.

                                          SIR THOMAS WYATT

Now Let Us Kiss

Now let us kiss; would you be gone?
Manners at least allow me one:
Blush you at this? pretty one stay,
And I will take that kiss away,
Thus with a second; and that too
A third wipes off; so will we go
To numbers that the stars out run,
And all the atoms in the sun:

For though we kiss 'till Phoebus ray
Sink in the seas, and kissing stay
'Till his bright beams return again,
There can of all but one remain:
And if for one good manners call,
In one, good manners grant me all.
Are kisses all? they but forerun
Another duty to be done:
What would you of that minstrel say,
That tunes his pipes and will not play?
Say, what are blossoms in their prime,
That ripen not in harvest time?
Or what are buds that ne'er disclose,
The long'd-for sweetness of the rose?
So kisses to a lover's guest
Are invitations, not the feast.

                              THOMAS RANDOLPH

The Kiss

Give me, my love, that billing kiss
    I taught you one delicious night,
When, turning epicures in bliss,
    We tried inventions of delight.

Come, gently steal my lips along,
    And let your lips in murmurs move, –
Ah, no! – again – that kiss was wrong –
    How can you be so dull, my love?

'Cease, cease!' the blushing girl replied –
    And in her milky arms she caught me –
'How can you thus your pupil chide;
    You know 'twas in the dark you taught me!'

                              THOMAS MOORE

Begging Another

For love's sake, kiss me once again!
I long, and should not beg in vain.
Here's none to spy or see;
Why do you doubt or stay?
I'll taste as lightly as the bee,
That doth but touch his flower, and flies away.
Once more, and faith, I will be gone —
Can he that loves ask less than one?
Nay, you may err in this,
And all your bounty wrong:
This could be called but half a kiss;
What we're but once to do, we should do long.

I will but mend the last, and tell
Where, how, it would have relished well;
Join lip to lip, and try:
Each suck the other's breath,
And whilst our tongues perplexèd lie,
Let who will think us dead, or wish our death!

BEN JONSON

A White Rose

The red rose whispers of passion,
  And the white rose breathes of love;
O, the red rose is a falcon,
  And the white rose is a dove.

But I send you a cream-white rosebud
  With a flush on its petal tips;
For the love that is purest and sweetest
  Has a kiss of desire on the lips.

JOHN BOYLE O'REILLY

The Kiss

'I saw you take his kiss!' ''Tis true.'
  'O, modesty!' ''Twas strictly kept:
'He thought me asleep; at least, I know
  'He thought I thought he thought I slept.'

COVENTRY PATMORE

The Look

Strephon kissed me in the spring,
  Robin in the fall,
But Colin only looked at me
  And never kissed at all.

Strephon's kiss was lost in jest,
  Robin's lost in play,
But the kiss in Colin's eyes
  Haunts me night and day.

SARA TEASDALE

The Kiss Alone

Come hither, womankind and all their worth,
Give me thy kisses as I call them forth.
Give me the billing kiss, that of the dove,
  A kiss of love;
The melting kiss, a kiss that doth consume
  To a perfume;
The extract kiss, of every sweet a part,
  A kiss of art;
The kiss which ever stirs some new delight,
  A kiss of might;

The twaching smacking kiss, and when you cease,
   A kiss of peace;
The music kiss, crochet-and-quaver time;
   The kiss of rhyme;
The kiss of eloquence, which doth belong
   Unto the tongue;
The kiss of all the sciences in one,
   The Kiss alone.
So, 'tis enough.

EDWARD HERBERT, LORD CHERBURY

'Tis Not To Be Spoke

I swear, I love you with my first virgin-fondness;
I live all in you, and I die without you:
At your approach my heart beats fast within me;
A pleasing trembling thrills thro' all my blood,
Whene'er you touch me with your melting hand:
But when you kiss, oh! 'tis not to be spoke!

ANONYMOUS

A Long, Long Kiss

A long, long kiss, a kiss of youth, and love;
   And beauty, all concentrating like rays
Into one focus, kindled from above;
   Such kisses as belong to early days,
Where heart, and soul, and sense, in concert move,
   And the blood's lava, and the pulse a blaze,
Each kiss a heart-quake – for a kiss's strength,
I think, it must be reckoned by its length.

By length, I mean duration; theirs endured
    Heaven knows how long – no doubt they never
        reckoned;
And if they had, they could not have secured
    The sum of their sensations to a second:
They had not spoken; but they felt allured,
    As if their souls and lips each other beckoned,
Which, being joined, like swarming bees they clung –
Their hearts the flowers from whence the honey sprung.

They were alone, but not alone as they
    Who shut in chambers think it loneliness;
The silent ocean, and the starlit bay,
    The twilight glow, which momently grew less,
The voiceless sands, and dropping caves, that lay
    Around them, made them to each other press,
As if there were no life beneath the sky
Save theirs, and that their life could never die.

They feared no eyes nor ears on that lone beach,
    They felt no terrors from the night; they were
All in all to each other; though their speech
    Was broken words, they thought a language there –
And all the burning tongues the passions teach
    Found in one sigh the best interpreter
Of nature's oracle – first love – that all
Which Eve has left her daughters since her fall.

GEORGE GORDON, LORD BYRON

Amphytrion

(EXTRACT)

How could I dwell for ever on these lips!
Oh! I could kiss 'em pale with eagerness!
So soft, by heaven! and such a juicy sweet,
That ripened peaches have not half their flavour.

JOHN DRYDEN

They Kissed With Such A Fervour

They kissed with such a fervour
And gave such furious earnest of their flames
That their eyes sparkled, and their mantling blood
Flew flushing over their faces.

JOHN DRYDEN

I Abhor The Slimy Kiss

I abhor the slimy kiss,
(which to me most loathsome is.)
Those lips please me which are placed
Close, but not too strictly laced:
Yielding I would have them; yet
Not a wimbling tongue admit:
What should poking-sticks make there,
When the ruff is set elsewhere ?

ROBERT HERRICK

Kissing Her Hair

Kissing her hair I sat against her feet,
Wove and unwove it, wound and found it sweet;
Made fast therewith her hands, drew down her eyes,
Deep as deep flowers and dreamy like dim skies;
With her own tresses bound and found her fair,
    Kissing her hair.

Sleep were no sweeter than her face to me,
Sleep of cold sea-bloom under the cold sea;
What pain could get between my face and hers?
What new sweet thing would love not relish worse?
Unless, perhaps, white death had kissed me there,
    Kissing her hair?

ALGERNON CHARLES SWINBURNE

Summum Bonum

All the breath and the bloom of the year in the bag of one bee;
All the wonder and wealth of the mine in the heart of one gem:
In the core of one pearl all the shade and the shine of the sea:
Breath and bloom, shade and shine, – wonder, wealth, and
    – how far above them –
      Truth, that's brighter than gem,
      Trust, that's purer than pearl –
Brightest truth, purest trust in the universe –
      All were for me in the kiss of one girl.

ROBERT BROWNING

Marriage Alamode

(EXTRACT)

I felt the while a pleasing kind of smart,
The kiss went tingling to my panting heart:
When it was gone, the sense of it did stay;
The sweetness cling'd upon my lips all day,
Like drops of honey, loath to fall away.

JOHN DRYDEN

To Electra

I dare not ask a kiss;
    I dare not beg a smile;
Lest having that or this,
    I might grow proud the while.

No, no, the utmost share
    Of my desire shall be,
Only to kiss that air
    That lately kissed thee.

ROBERT HERRICK

LOVE'S TYRANNY

Love Armed

Love in fantastic triumph sate,
　　Whilst bleeding hearts around him flowed,
For whom fresh pains he did create,
　　And strange tyrannic power he showed
From thy bright eyes he took his fires
　　Which round about in sport he hurled,
But t'was from mine he took desires,
　　Enough t'undo the amorous world.

From me he took his sighs and tears,
　　From thee his pride and cruelty:
From me his languishments and fears,
　　And ev'ry killing dart from thee.
Thus thou and I the god have armed,
　　And set him up a deity:
But my poor heart alone is harmed
　　While thine the victor is and free.

APHRA BEHN

Cupid Lost

Late in the forest I did Cupid see
　　Cold, wet, and crying he had lost his way,
　　And being blind was farther like to stray:
　　Which sight a kind compassion bred in me,

I kindly took, and dried him, while that he
　　Poor child complained he starvèd was with stay,
　　And pined for want of his accustomed play,
　　For none in that wild place his host would be,

I glad was of his finding, thinking sure
   This service should my freedom still procure,
   And in my arms I took him then unharmed,

Carrying him safe unto a myrtle bower
   But in the way he made me feel his power,
   Burning my heart who had him kindly warmed.

LADY MARY WROTH

Sonnet

Love banished heaven, in earth was held in scorn,
Wand'ring abroad in need and beggary;
And wanting friends tho' of a goddess born,
Yet craved the alms of such as passèd by:
I, like a man devout and charitable,
Clothed the naked, lodged this wand'ring guest,
With sighs and tears still furnishing his table,
With what might make the miserable blest:
But this ungrateful, for my good desert,
Enticed my thoughts against me to conspire,
Who gave consent to steal away my heart,
And set my breast, his lodging, on a fire,
   Well, well, my friends, when beggars grow thus bold
   No marvel then tho' charity grow cold.

MICHAEL DRAYTON

The Vain Advice

   Ah, gaze not on those eyes! forbear
   That soft enchanting voice to hear:
Not looks of basilisks give surer death,
Nor Syrens sing with more destructive breath.

Fly, if thy freedom thou'dst maintain,
Alas! I feel th'advice is vain!
A heart, whose safety but in flight does lie,
Is too far lost to have the power to fly.

CATHERINE COCKBURN

To Cupid

Child, with many a childish wile,
Timid look, and blushing smile,
Downy wings to steal thy way,
Gilded bow, and quiver gay,
Who in thy simple mien would trace
The tyrant of the human race?

Who is he whose flinty heart
Hath not felt the flying dart?
Who is he that from the wound
Hath not pain and pleasure found?
Who is he that hath not shed
Curse and blessing on thy head?

JOANNA BAILLIE

Thou Rob'st Me

Thou rob'st my days of bus'ness and delights!
Of sleep, thou rob'st my nights:
Ah! lovely thief! what wilt thou do?
What! rob me – of heav'n too!
Thou e'en my prayers do'st steal from me,
For I, with wild idolatry!
Begin to God! and end them all to thee.

ABRAHAM COWLEY

Liberty?

from URANIA

Did I boast of liberty?
    'Twas an insolency vain
I do only look on thee,
    And I captive am again.

LADY MARY WROTH

Epistle From Elivira (A Spanish Lady) To Her Lover (A Native of Portugal)

(EXTRACT)

Fool that I was, and to the future blind!
Love banished reason from my erring mind;
Love tempted me to break thro' moral rules,
And scorn the rigid laws of men and schools;
Frail was my heart, too strong the conflict prov'd,
When Osmyn flattered and Elvira loved;
Pride, shame, and honour, strove in vain to plead –
Seduced by love, my ruin was decreed.

Yet, dear associate! (for thou still art dear,
Formed to delight mine eye, and charm mine ear,)
In my fond heart thou has unaltered power,
And him whom I upbraid, I still adore;
Wronged as I am, and deeply as I grieve,
If Osmyn pleads, Elvira must forgive.

*   *   *

This is thy work, imperious love! Whose sway
Makes youth and sensibility thy prey,
Rends me from all the blessing life could give,
And blasts the wreath immortal fame might weave.
On my sad tomb no record must appear,
Silence will wear the best expression there –

To long oblivion by my name consigned,
So shall no cheek for me be tinged with shame.
So shall no rigid censor curse my name.

SOPHIA BURRELL

To One Who Said I Must Not Love

Bid the fond mother spill her infant's blood,
The hungry epicure not think of food;
Bid the Antarctic touch the Arctic pole:
When these obey, I'll force love from my soul.
As light and heat compose the genial sun,
So love and I essentially are one:
Ere your advice, a thousand ways I tried
To ease the inherent pain, but 'twas denied,
Though I resolved, and grieved, and almost died.
Then I would needs dilute the mighty flame:
The modish remedy I tried in vain,
One thought of him contracts it all again.
Wearied at last, cursed Hymen's aid I chose,
But find the fettered soul has no repose.
Now I'm a double slave to love and vows:
As if my former sufferings were too small,
I've made the guiltless torture criminal.
Ere this, I gave a loose to fond desire,
Durst smile, be kind, look, languish and admire,
With wishing sighs fan the transporting fire.
But now these soft allays are so like sin,
I'm forced to keep the mighty anguish in;
Check my too tender thoughts and rising sighs,
As well as eager arms and longing eyes.
My kindness to his picture I refrain,
Nor now embrace the lifeless, lovely swain.
To press the charming shade, though through a glass,
Seems a platonic breach of Hymen's laws;
Thus nicely fond, I only stand and gaze,
View the dear, conquering form that forced my fate,

Till I become as motionless as that.
My sinking limbs deny their wonted aid:
Fainting, I lean against my frighted maid,
Whose cruel care restores my sense and pain,
For soon as I have life I love again,
And with the fated softness strive in vain.
Distorted nature shakes at the control,
With strong revulsions rends my struggling soul;
Each vital string cracks with th'unequal strife,
Departing love racks like departing life;
Yet there the sorrow ceases with the breath,
But love each day renews th'torturing scene of death.

                                        SARAH EGERTON

Golden Fetters

Whilst I behold thy glittering golden hairs
Dishevelled thus, waving about thy ears,
And see those locks thus loosèd and undone
For their more pomp to sport them in the sun,
Love takes those threads and weaves them with that art
He knits a thousand knots about my heart
And with such skill and cunning he them sets,
My soul lies taken in those lovely nets,
Making me cry, 'Fair prison, that dost hold
My heart in fetters wrought of burnished gold.'

                                        JAMES MABBE

Pastoral Dialogue

Remember when you love, from that same hour
Your peace you put into your lover's power;
From that same hour from him you laws receive,
And as he shall ordain, you joy, or grieve,

Hope, fear, laugh, weep; reason aloof does stand,
Disabled both to act, and to command.
Oh cruel fetter! rather wish to feel
On your soft limbs, the galling weight of steel;
Rather to bloody wounds oppose your breast.
No ill, by which the body can be pressed
You will so sensible a torment find
As shackles on your captived mind.
The mind from heaven its high descent did draw,
And brooks uneasily any other law
Than what from reason dictated shall be.
Reason, a kind of innate deity,
Which only can adapt to ev'ry soul
A yoke so fit and light, that the control
All liberty excells; so sweet a sway,
The same 'tis to be happy, and obey;
Commands so wise, and with rewards so dressed,
That the according soul replies, 'I'm blessed'.

ANNE KILLIGREW

A Valentine

(EXTRACT)

When to love's influence woman yields,
She loves for life! and daily feels
Progressive tenderness! – each hour
Confirms, extends, the tyrant's power!
Her lover is her god! her fate! –
Vain pleasures, riches, worldly state,
Are trifles all! – each sacrifice
Becomes a dear and valued prize,
If made for him, e'en tho' he proves
Forgetful of their former loves!

ELIZABETH TREFUSIS

Love

Love's sooner felt, than seen; his substance thin
Betwixt those snowy mounts in ambush lies:
Oft in the eyes he spreads his subtle ginne;
He therefore soonest wins that fastest flies.
Fly thence, my dear, fly fast, my Thomalin:
Who him encounters once, for ever dies:
    But if he lurk between the ruddy lips,
    Unhappy soul, that thence his nectar sips,
While down into his heart the sugared poison slips!

Oft in a voice he creeps down through the ear:
Oft from a blushing cheek he lights his fire:
Oft shrouds his golden flame in likest hair:
Oft in a soft-smooth skin doth close retire:
Oft in a smile: oft in a silent tear:
And if all fail, yet virtue's self he'll hire:
    Himself's a dart, when nothing else can move.
    Who then the captive soul can well reprove,
When love, and virtue's self become the darts of love?

PHINEAS FLETCHER

Hopes In Vain

Kind are her answers,
But her performance keeps no day;
    Breaks time, as dancers
From their own music when they stray.
All her free favours and smooth words
    Wing my hopes in vain.
Oh did ever voice so sweet but only feign?
    Can true love yield to such delay
    Converting joy to pain?

Lost is our freedom
When we submit to women so.
 Why do we need them
When in their best they work our woe?
 There is no wisdom
Can alter ends, by fate prefixed.
Oh why is the good of man with evil mixed?
 Never were days yet callèd two
 But one night went betwixt.

THOMAS CAMPION

Fire And Fetters

When I lie burning in thy eye,
 Or freezing in thy breast,
What martyrs, in wished flames that die,
 Are half so pleased or blest?

When thy soft accents, through mine ear,
 Into my soul do fly,
What angel would not quit his sphere
 To hear such harmony?

Or when the kiss thou gav'st me last
 My soul stole, in its breath,
What life would sooner be embraced
 Than so desired a death?

Then think not freedom I desire,
 Or would my fetters leave,
Since, Phoenix-like, I from this fire
 Both life and youth receive.

THOMAS STANLEY

Love's Servile Lot

Love, mistress, is of many minds,
   Yet few know whom they serve,
They reckon least how little love
   Their service doth deserve.

The will she robbeth from the wit
   The sense from reason's lore,
She is delightful in the rine,
   Corrupted in the core.

She shroudeth vice in virtue's veil,
   Pretending good in ill,
She offereth joy, affordeth grief,
   A kiss where she doth kill.

A honey-shower rains from her lips,
   Sweet lights shine in her face,
She hath the blush of a virgin mind,
   The mind of viper's race.

She makes them seek, yet fear to find;
   To find, but not enjoy:
In many frowns some gliding smiles
   She yields to more annoy.

She woos thee to come near her fire,
   Yet doth she draw it from thee,
Far off she makes thy heart to fry,
   And yet to freeze within thee.

She letteth fall some luring baits
   For fools to gather up;
Too sweet, too sour, to every taste
   She tempereth her cup.

Soft souls she binds in tender twist,
   Small flies in spinner's web;
She sets afloat some luring streams
   But makes them soon to ebb.

Her watery eyes have burning force;
    Her floods and flames conspire:
Tears kindle sparks, sobs fuel are,
    And sighs do blow her fire.

May never was the month of love,
    For May is full of flowers,
But rather April, wet by kind,
    For love is full of showers.

Like tyrant, cruel wound she gives,
    Like surgeon, salve she lends;
But salve and sore have equal force,
    For death is both their ends.

With soothing words, enthrallèd souls
    She chains in servile bands;
Her eye in silence has a speech
    Which eye best understands.

Her little sweet hath many sours
    Short hap immortal harms;
Her loving looks are murd'ring darts,
    Her songs bewitching charms.

Like winter rose and summer ice
    Her joys are still untimely;
Before her hope, behind remorse:
    Fair first, in fine unseemly.

Moods, passions, fancies, jealous fits,
    Attend upon her train:
She yieldeth rest without repose,
    And heaven in hellish pain.

Her house is sloth, her door deceit,
    And slippery hope her stairs;
Unbashful boldness bids her guests,
    And every vice repairs.

Her diet is of such delights
    As please till they be past;
But then the poison kills the hart,
    That did entice the taste.

Her sleep in sin doth end in wrath,
    Remorse rings her awake;
Death calls her up, shame drives her out,
    Despairs her up-shot make.

Plow not the seas, sow not the sands,
    Leave off you idle pain;
Seek other mistress for your minds,
    Love's service is in vain.

ROBERT SOUTHWELL

Love Is A Sickness

Love is a sickness full of woes,
    All remedies refusing;
A plant that most with cutting grows,
    Most barren with best using.
      Why so?
More we enjoy it, more it dies,
    If not enjoyed, it sighing cries,
      Heigh-ho!

Love is a torment of the mind,
    A tempest everlasting;
And Jove hath made it of a kind
    Not well, nor full nor fasting.
      Why so?
More we enjoy it, more it dies,
    If not enjoyed, it sighing cries,
      Heigh-ho!

SAMUEL DANIEL

Upon Love

Love scorched my finger, but did spare
    The burning of my heart:
To signify, in love my share
    Should be a little part.

Little I love; but if that he
    Would but that heat recall:
That joint to ashes burnt should be,
    Ere I would love at all.

                ROBERT HERRICK

The Penalty Of Love

If love should count you worthy, and should deign
One day to seek your door and be your guest,
Pause! ere you draw the bolt and bid him rest,
If in your old content you would remain.
For not alone he enters: in his train
Are angels of the mists, the lonely quest,
Dreams of the unfulfilled and unpossessed,
And sorrow, and life's immemorial pain.
He wakes desires you never may forget,
He shows you stars you never saw before,
He makes you share with him, for evermore,
The burden of the world's divine regret.
How wise were you to open not! – and yet,
How poor if you should turn him from the door.

                SIDNEY ROYSE LYSAGHT

Farewell, False Love!

Farewell, false love! the oracle of lies,
A mortal foe, and enemy to rest;
An envious boy, from whom all cares arise;
A bastard vile, a beast with rage possessed,
A way of error, a temple full of treason:
In all effects, contrary unto reason.

A poisoned serpent covered all with flowers,
Mother of sighs and murderer of repose;
A sea of sorrows from whence are drawn such showers
As moisture lend to every grief that grows;
A school of guile, a net of deep deceit,
A gilded hook that holds a poisoned bait.

A fortress foiled, which reason did defend,
A siren song, a fever of the mind,
A maze wherein affection finds no end,
A raging cloud that runs before the wind,
A substance like the shadow of the sun,
A goal of grief for which the wisest run.

A quenchless fire, a nurse of trembling fear,
A path that leads to peril and mishap,
A true retreat of sorrow and despair,
An idle boy that sleeps in pleasure's lap,
A deep mistrust of that which certain seems,
A hope of that which reason doubtful deems.

SIR WALTER RALEGH

Freedom

Now heaven be thanked. I am out of love again!
I have been long a slave, and now am free:
I have been tortured, and am eased of pain:
I have been blind, and now my eyes can see:
I have been lost, and now my way lies plain:
I have been caged, and now I hold the key:
I have been mad, and now at last am sane:
I am wholly I that was but half of me.
So a free man, my dull proud path I plod,
Who, tortured, blind, mad, caged, was once a God.

                                        JAN STRUTHER

Days Spent In Vain

I curse the time, wherein these lips of mine
Did pray or praise the dame that was unkind:
I curse both leaf, and ink, and every line
My hand hath writ, in hope to move her mind:
I curse her hollow heart and flattering eyes,
Whose sly deceit did cause my mourning cries:
I curse the sugared speech and siren's song,
Wherewith so oft she hath bewitched mine ear:
I curse my foolish will, that stayed so long,
And took delight to bide twixt hope and fear:
I curse the hour, wherein I first began
By loving looks to prove a witless man:
I curse those days which I have spent in vain,
By serving such an one as recks no right:
I curse each cause of all my secret pain,
Though love to hear the same have small delight:
And since the heavens my freedom now restore,
Henceforth I'll live at ease, and love no more.

                                        THOMAS WATSON

Farewell, Love

Farewell, love, and all thy laws for ever:
Thy baited hooks shall tangle me no more;
Senec and Plato call me from thy lore,
To perfect wealth my wit for to endeavour.
In blind error when I did persever,
Thy sharp repulse, that pricketh ay so sore,
Hath taught me to set in trifles no store,
And scape forth, since liberty is lever.
Therefore, farewell: go trouble younger hearts,
And in me claim no more authority;
With idle youth go use thy property,
And thereon spend thy many brittle darts;
For hitherto though I have lost all my time,
Me lusteth no longer rotten boughs to climb.

SIR THOMAS WYATT

Remedia Amoris

TO HENRY CROMWELL ESQ.

Love and the gout invade the idle brain,
Bus'ness prevents the passion and the pain:
Ceres and Bacchus, envious of our ease,
Blow up the flame, and heighten the disease.
Withdraw the fuel, and the fire goes out;
Hard beds, and fasting, cure both love and gout.

ELIZABETH THOMAS

The Question Answered

What is it men in women do require?
The lineaments of Gratified Desire.
What is it women do in men require?
The lineaments of Gratified Desire.

WILLIAM BLAKE

Did Not

'Twas a new feeling – something more
Than we had dared to own before,
   Which then we hid not;
We saw it in each other's eye,
And wished, in every half-breathed sigh,
   To speak, but did not.

She felt my lips' impassioned touch –
'Twas the first time I dared so much,
   And yet she chid not;
But whispered o'er my burning brow,
'Oh, do you doubt I love you now?'
   Sweet soul! I did not.

Warmly I felt her bosom thrill,
I pressed it closer, closer still,
   Though gently bid not;
Till – oh! the world hath seldom heard
Of lovers, who so nearly erred,
   And yet, who did not.

THOMAS MOORE

After You Speak

After you speak
And what you meant
Is plain,
My eyes
Meet yours that mean,
With your cheeks and hair,
Something more wise,
More dark,
And far different.
Even so the lark
Loves dust
And nestles in it
The minute
Before he must
Soar in lone flight
So far,
Like a black star
He seems –
A mote
Of singing dust
Afloat
Above,
That dreams
And sheds no light.
I know your lust
Is love.

EDWARD THOMAS

To Anthea

Ah my Anthea! Must my heart still break?
(Love makes me write, what shame forbids to speak.)
Give me a kiss, and to that kiss a score;
Then to that twenty, add an hundred more:

A thousand to that hundred: so kiss on,
To make that thousand up a million.
Treble that million, and when that is done,
Let's kiss afresh, as when we first begun.
But yet, though love likes well such scenes as these,
There is an act that will more fully please:
Kissing and glancing, soothing, all make way
But to the acting of this private play:
Name it I would; but being blushing red,
The rest I'll speak, when we meet both in bed.

ROBERT HERRICK

The Ecstasy

(EXTRACT)

Where, like a pillow on a bed,
    A pregnant bank swelled up, to rest
The violet's reclining head,
    Sat we two, one another's best.
Our hands were firmly cemented
    With a fast balm, which thence did spring,
Our eye-beams twisted, and did thread
    Our eyes, upon one double string;
So to entergraft our hands, as yet
    Was all the means to make us one,
And pictures in our eyes to get
    Was all our propagation.
As, 'twixt two equal armies, fate
    Suspends uncertain victory,
Our souls, which to advance their state,
    Were gone out, hung 'twixt her and me.
And whilst our souls negotiate there,
    We like sepulchral statues lay;
All day the same our postures were,
    And we said nothing all the day . . .

JOHN DONNE

Wild Nights!

Wild nights! Wild nights!
Were I with thee,
Wild nights should be
Our luxury!

Futile in the winds
To a heart in port,
Done with the compass,
Done with the chart.

Rowing in Eden!
Ah! the sea!
Might I but moor
Tonight in thee!

EMILY DICKINSON

Love's First Approach

Strephon I saw, and started at the sight,
And interchangeably looked red and white;
I felt my blood run swiftly to my heart,
And a chill trembling seize each outward part:
By breath grew short, my pulse did quicker beat,
My heart did heave, as it would change its seat:
A faint cold sweat o'er all my body spread,
A giddy megrim* wheeled about my head:
When for the reason of this change I sought,
I found my eyes had all the mischief wrought;
For they my soul to Strephon had betrayed,
And my weak heart his willing victim made:
The traitors, conscious of the treason
They had committed 'gainst my reason,
Looked down with such a bashful guilty fear,
As made their fault to every eye appear.
Tho' the first fatal look too much had done,

The lawless wanderers would still gaze on,
Kind looks repeat, and glances steal, till they
Had looked my liberty and heart away:
Great love, I yield; send no more darts in vain,
I am already fond of my soft chain;
Proud of my fetters, so pleased with my state,
That I the very thought of freedom hate.
O mighty love! thy art and power join,
To make his frozen breast as warm as mine;
But if thou try'st, and can'st not make him kind,
In love such pleasant, real sweets I find;
That though attended with despair it be,
'Tis better still than a wild liberty.

'EPHELIA'

*headache

Between Your Sheets

Between your sheets you soundly sleep
Nor dream of vigils that we lovers keep
While all the night, I waking sigh your name,
The tender sound does every nerve inflame,
Imagination shows me all your charms,
The plenteous silken hair, and waxen arms,
The well-turned neck, and snowy rising breast
And all the beauties that supinely rest
      between your sheets.

Ah Lindamira, could you see my heart,
How fond, how true, how free from fraudful art,
The warmest glances poorly do explain
The eager wish, the melting throbbing pain
Which through my very blood and soul I feel,
Which you cannot believe nor I reveal,
Which every metaphor must render less
And yet (methinks) which I could well express
      between your sheets.

LADY MARY WORTLEY MONTAGU

Steaming

The library is steaming, heat
licked as some old barn gone brittle
with electric storms. The walls
cave inward from us. Someone
smokes. I turn my pages. Everyone
drinks tea at four
o'clock. At six I watch you coming in. You melt
the doorway, tread the carpet white hot. Heat
runs from the walls. My cheeks catch flame.

Outside, on the library steps, the windows
glow out gold to us, lighting, in a half way,
my face, steaming your grandfather's glasses.

JEAN HANFF KORELITZ

Desire Gratified

Abstinence sows sand all over
The ruddy limbs and flaming hair,
But Desire Gratified
Plants fruits of life and beauty there.

WILLIAM BLAKE

The Globe Of Fire

As Corydon went shiv'ring by,
Sylvia a ball of snow let fly.
Which straight a globe of fire became,
And put the shepherd in a flame;
Cupid now break thy darts and bow,
Sylvia can all thy feats outdo,
Fire us with ice, burn us with snow.

MARY MONK

Second Thoughts

I thought of leaving her for a day
In town, it was such iron winter
At Durdans, the garden frosty clay,
The woods as dry as any splinter,
The sky congested. I would break
From the deep, lethargic, country air
To the shining lamps, to the clash of the play,
And to-morrow, wake
Beside her, a thousand things to say.
I planned – O more – I had almost started; –
I lifted her face in my hands to kiss, –
A face in a border of fox's fur,
For the bitter black wind had stricken her,
And she wore it – her soft hair straying out
Where it buttoned against the gray, leather snout:
In an instant we should have parted;
But at sight of the delicate world within
That fox-fur collar, from brow to chin,
At sight of those wonderful eyes from the mine,
Coal pupils, an iris of glittering spa,
And the wild, ironic, defiant shine
As of a creature behind a bar
One has captured, and, when three lives are past,
May hope to reach the heart of at last,
All that, and the love at her lips, combined
To shew me what folly it were to miss
A face with such thousand things to say,
And beside these, such thousand more to spare,
For the shining lamps, for the clash of the play –
O madness; not for a single day
Could I leave her! I stayed behind.

MICHAEL FIELD

Under The Willow-Shades

Under the willow-shades they were
    Free from the eye-sight of the sun,
For no intruding beam could there
    Peep through to spy what things were done:
        Thus sheltered they unseen did lie,
        Surfeiting on each other's eye;
Defended by the willow-shades alone,
The sun's heat they defied and cooled their own.

Whilst they did embrace unspied,
    The conscious willow seemed to smile,
That them with privacy supplied,
    Holding the door, as 't were, the while;
        And when their dalliances were o'er,
        The willows, to oblige them more,
Bowing, did seem to say, as they withdrew,
'We can supply you with a cradle too.'

                    SIR WILLIAM DAVENANT

Corn Rigs

It was upon a Lammas night,
    When corn rigs are bonie,
Beneath the moon's unclouded light
    I held awa to Annie:
The time flew by, wi' tentless heed,
    Till 'tween the late and early;
Wi' sma' persuasion she agreed,
    To see me thro' the barley.

    Corn rigs, an' barley rigs,
        An' corn rigs are bonie:
    O, I'll ne'er forget that happy night,
        Amang the rigs wi' Annie.

The sky was blue, the wind was still,
    The moon was shining clearly;
I set her down, wi' right good will,
    Amang the rigs o' barley:
I ken't her heart was a' my ain;
    I lov'd her most sincerely;
I kiss'd her owre and owre again,
    Amang the rigs o' barley.

I lock'd her in my fond embrace;
    Her heart was beating rarely:
My blessings on that happy place,
    Amang the rigs o' barley!
But by the moon and stars so bright,
    That shone that night so clearly!
She ay shall bless that happy night,
    Amang the rigs o' barley.

I hae been blythe wi' comrades dear;
    I hae been merry drinking;
I hae been joyfu' gath'rin' gear;
    I hae been happy thinking:
But a' the pleasures e'er I saw,
    Tho' three times doubl'd fairly,
That happy night was worth them a',
    Amang the rigs o' barley.

ROBERT BURNS

A Prayer

Again!
Come, give, yield all your strength to me!
From far a low word breathes on the breaking brain
Its cruel calm, submission's misery,
Gentling her awe as to a soul predestined.
Cease, silent love! My doom!

Blind me with your dark nearness, O have mercy,
   beloved enemy of my will!
I dare not withstand the cold touch that I dread.
Draw from me still
My slow life! Bend deeper on me, threatening head,
Proud by my downfall, remembering, pitying
Him who is, him who was!

Again!
Together, folded by the night, they lay on earth.
   I hear
From far her low word breathe on my breaking brain.
Come! I yield. Bend deeper upon me! I am here.
Subduer, do not leave me! Only joy, only anguish,
Take me, save me, soothe me, O spare me!

JAMES JOYCE

Ah Me, If I Grew Sweet To Man

Ah me, if I grew sweet to man
It was but as a rose that can
No longer keep the breath that heaves
And swells among its folded leaves.

The pressing fragrance would unclose
The flower, and I become a rose,
That unimpeachable and fair
Planted its sweetness in the air.

No art I used men's love to draw;
I lived but by my being's law,
As roses are by heaven designed
To bring the honey to the wind.

MICHAEL FIELD

Now

Out of your whole life give but a moment!
All of your life that has gone before,
All to come after it, – so you ignore,
So you make perfect the present, – condense,
In a rapture of rage, for perfection's endowment,
Thought and feeling and soul and sense –
Merged in a moment which gives me at last
You around me for once, you beneath me, above me –
Me – sure that despite of time future, time past, –
This tick of our life-time's one moment you love me!
How long such suspension may linger? Ah, sweet –
The moment eternal – just that and no more –
When ecstasy's utmost we clutch at the core
While cheeks burn, arms open, eyes shut and lips meet!

ROBERT BROWNING

Lilies In The Fire

(EXTRACT)

I am ashamed, you wanted me not to-night.
And it is always so, you sigh against me.
Your brightness dims when I draw too near, and my free
Fire enters you like frost, like a cruel blight.

And now I know, so I must be ashamed;
You love me while I hover tenderly
Like moonbeams kissing you; but the body of me
Closing upon you in the lightning-flamed

Moment, destroys you, you are just destroyed.
Humiliation deep to me, that all my best
Soul's naked lightning, which should sure attest
God stepping through our loins in one bright stride

Means but to you a burden of dead flesh
Heavy to bear, even heavy to uprear
Again from earth, like lilies flagged and sere
Upon the floor, that erst stood up so fresh.

D.H. LAWRENCE

The Disappointment

One day the amorous Lysander,
By an impatient passion swayed,
Surprised fair Cloris, that loved maid,
Who could defend herself no longer.
All things did with his love conspire;
The gilded planet of the day,
In his gay chariot drawn by fire,
Was now descending to the sea,
And left no light to guide the world,
But what from Cloris brighter eyes was hurled.

In a lone thicket made for love,
Silent as yielding maid's consent,
She with a charming languishment,
Permits his force, yet gently strove;
Her hands his bosom softly meet,
But not to put him back designed,
Rather to draw 'em on inclined:
Whilst he lay trembling at her feet,
Resistance 'tis in vain to show;
She wants the power to say – Ah! What d'ye do?

Her bright eyes sweet, and yet severe,
Where love and shame confusedly strive,
Fresh vigour to Lysander give;
And breathing faintly in his ear,
She cried – *Cease, cease – your vain desire,*
Or I'll call out – What would you do?
My dearer honour ev'n to you
I cannot, must not give – Retire,
Or take this life, whose chiefest part
I gave you with the conquest of my heart.

But he as much unused to fear,
As he was capable of love,
The blessed minutes to improve,
Kisses her mouth, her neck, her hair;
Each touch her new desire alarms.
His burning trembling hand he prest
Upon her swelling snowy breast,
While she lay panting in his arms.
All her unguarded beauties lie
The spoils and trophies of the energy.

Her balmy lips countring his,
As their souls, are joined;
Both in transports unconfined
Extend themselves upon the moss.
Cloris half dead and breathless lay;
Her soft eyes cast a humid light,
Such as divides the day and night;
Or falling stars, whose fires decay:
And now no signs of life she shows,
But what in short-breathed sighs returns and goes.

He saw how at her length she lay;
He saw her rising bosom bare;
Her loose thin robes, though which appear
A shape designed for love and play;
Abandoned by her pride and shame.
She does her softest joys dispense,
Off'ring her virgin-innocence
A victim to love's sacred flame;
While the o'er-ravished shepherd lies
Unable to perform the sacrifice.

Ready to taste a thousand Joys,
The too transported hapless swain
Found the vast pleasure turned to pain;
Pleasure which too much love destroys:
The willing garments by he laid,
And heaven all opened to his view,
Mad to possess, himself he threw
On the defenceless lovely maid.
But Oh what envying God conspires
To snatch his power, yet leave him the desire.

Nature's support, (without whose aid
She can no humane being give)
Itself now wants the art to live;
Faintness its slackened nerves invade:
In vain th'enraged youth essayed
To call its fleeting vigour back,
No motion 'twill from motion take;
Excess of love is love betrayed:
In vain he toils, in vain commands,
Then I sensible fell weeping in his hand.

In this so amorous cruel strife,
Where love and fate were too severe
The poor Lysander in despair
Renounced his reason with his life
Now all the brisk and active fire
That should the nobler part inflame,
Serv'd to increase his rage and shame
And left no spark for new desire:
Not all her naked charms could move
Or calm that rage that had debauched his love.

Cloris returning from the trance
Which love and soft desire had bred,
Her timorous hand she gently laid
(Or guided by design or chance)
Soon that fabulous Priapus,
That potent god, as poets feign;
But never did young shepherdess,
Gath'ring of fern upon the plain,
Nimbly draw her fingers back,
Finding beneath the verdant leaves a snake.

APHRA BEHN

The Choice Of Valentines

'Oh not so fast,' my ravished mistress cries,
'Lest my content, that on thy life relies
Be brought too soon from his delightful seat,
And me unawares of hoped bliss defeat.
Together let our equal motions stir,
Together let us live and die my dear,
Together let us march unto content,
And be consumed with one blandishment.'
As she prescribed, so kept we crotchet-time,
And every stroke in order like a chime.
Whilst she, that had preserved me by her pity,
Unto our music framed a groaning ditty.

Alas, alas, that love should be a sin,
Even now my bliss and sorrow doth begin.
Hold wide thy lap, my lovely Danaë,
And entertain the golden shower so free,
That trilling falls into thy treasury,
As April drops not half so pleasant be,
Nor Nilus overflow, to Egypt plains,
As this sweet stream, that all her joints embaynes;
With Oh, and Oh, she itching moves her hips,
And to and fro, full lightly starts and skips.
She jerks her legs, and sprawleth with her heels,
No tongue may tell the solace that she feels.
I faint, I yield; Oh death rock me asleep;
Sleep – sleep desire, entombèd in the deep.
'Not so my dear,' my dearest saint replied;
'For, from us yet thy spirit may not glide
Until the sinewy channels of our blood
Withhold their source from this imprisoned flood;
And then will we (that then will come too soon)
Dissolved lie as though our days were done.
The whilst I speak, my soul is fleeting hence,
And life forsakes his fleshy residence.
Stay, stay sweet joy, and leave me not forlorn,
Why shouldst thou fade, that art but newly born?
Stay but an hour; an hour is not so much,
But half an hour; if that thy haste be such:
Nay but a quarter; I will ask no more,
That thy departure (which torments me sore)
May be alightened with a little pause,
And take away this passion's sudden cause.
He hears me not, hard-hearted as he is:
He is the son of Time, and hates my bliss.
Time ne'er looks back, the rivers ne'er return;
A second spring must help me or I burn.'
'No, no, the well is dry that should refresh me,
The glass is run of all my destiny.
Nature of winter learneth nigardise,
Who, as he overbears the stream with ice,
That man nor beast may of their pleasance taste,
So shuts she up her conduit all in haste,

And will not let her nectar overflow,
Lest mortal men immortal joys should know.'
'Adieu unconstant love, to thy disport,
Adieu false mirth, and melody too-short.
Adieu faint-hearted instrument of lust,
That falsely hast betrayed our equal trust.
Henceforth no more will I implore thine aid,
Or thee, or men of cowardice upbraid.
My little dildo shall supply their kind:
A knave, that moves as light as leaves by wind;
That bendeth not, nor foldeth any deal,
But stands as stiff, as he were made of steel,
And plays at peacock twixt my legs right blithe,
And doeth my tickling assuage with many a sigh;
For, by Saint Runnion he'll refresh me well,
And never make my tender belly swell.'

THOMAS NASHE

I Have A Gentle Cock

I have a gentle* cock, croweth me day.
He doth me risen early my matins for to say.

I have a gentle cock, comen he is of gret†,
His comb is of red coral, his tail is of jet.

I have a gentle cock, comen he is of kinde°,
His comb is of red coral, his tail is of inde•.

His legges ben of asor*, so gentle and so smale,
His spores† arn of silver white into the wortewale°.

His eynen• are of crystal loken* all in aumber†,
And every night he percheth him in mine lady's chamber.

ANONYMOUS

*of good family   †great forebears   °(good) kin   •indigo
*azure   †spurs   °skin at the root of the spur   •eyes
*set   †amber

The Dream

From A VOYAGE TO THE ISLE OF LOVE

All trembling in my arms Aminta lay,
Defending of the bliss I strove to take;
Raising my rapture by her kind delay,
Her force so charming was and weak.
The soft resistance did betray the grant,
While I pressed on the heaven of my desires;
Her rising breasts with nimbler motions pant;
Her dying eyes assume new fires.
Now to the height of languishment she grows,
And still her looks new charms put on;
– Now the last mystery of love she knows,
We sigh, and kiss: I waked, and all was done.

'Twas but a dream, yet by my heart I knew,
Which still was panting, part of it was true:
Oh how I strove the rest to have believed;
Ashamed and angry to be undeceived!

APHRA BEHN

The Vine

I dreamed this mortal part of mine
Was metamorphosed to a vine;
Which crawling one and every way,
Enthralled my dainty Lucia.
Me thought, her long small legs and thighs
I with my tendrils did surprise;
Her belly, buttocks, and her waist
By now soft nervelets were embraced:
About her head I writhing hung,
And with rich clusters (hid among
The leaves) her temples I behung
So that my Lucia seemed to me

Young Bacchus ravished by his tree.
My curls about her neck did crawl,
And arms and hands they did enthral;
So that she could not freely stir,
(All parts there made one prisoner).
But when I crept with leaves to hide
Those parts, which maids keep unespied,
Such fleeting pleasures there I took,
That with the fancy I awoke;
And found (Ah me!) this flesh of mine
More like a stock, than like a vine.

ROBERT HERRICK

She Lay All Naked

She lay all naked in her bed,
    And I myself lay by;
No veil but curtains about her spread,
    No covering but I:
Her head upon her shoulders seeks
    To hang in careless wise,
And full of blushes was her cheek,
    And of wishes were her eyes.

Her blood still fresh into her face,
    As on a message came,
To say that in another place
    It meant another game,
Her cherry lip moist, plump and fair,
    Millions of kisses crown,
Which ripe and uncropped dangled there,
    And weigh the branches down.

Her breasts, that welled so plump and high
    Bred pleasant pain in me,
For all the world I do defy
    The like felicity;

Her thighs and belly, soft and fair,
 To me were only shown:
To have seen such meat, and not to have eat,
 Would have angered any stone.

Her knees lay upward gently bent,
 And all lay hollow under,
As if on easy terms, they meant
 To fall unforced asunder;
Just so the Cyprian Queen did lie,
 Expecting in her bower;
When too long stay had kept the boy
 Beyond his promised hour.

'Dull clown,' quoth she, 'why dost delay
 Such proferred bliss to take?
Canst thou find out no other way
 Similitudes to make?'
Mad with delight I thundering
 Throw my arms about her,
But pox upon't 'twas but a dream.
 And so I lay without her.

ANONYMOUS

The Vision To Electra

I dreamed we both were in a bed
Of roses, almost smothered:
The warmth and sweetness had me there
Made lovingly familiar:
But that I heard thy sweet breath say,
Faults done by night, will blush by day:
I kissed thee (panting) and I call
Night to the record! that was all.
But ah! if empty dreams so please,
Love give me more such nights as these.

ROBERT HERRICK

A Sonnet Of The Moon

Look how the pale queen of the silent night
Doth cause the ocean to attend upon her,
And he, as long as she is in his sight,
With his full tide is ready her to honour:
But when the silver wagon of the moon
Is mounted up so high he cannot follow,
The sea calls home his crystal waves to moan,
And with low ebb doth manifest his sorrow.
So you, that are the sovereign of my heart,
Have all my joys attending on your will:
My joys low ebbing when you do depart,
When you return, their tide my heart doth fill.
    So as you come, and as you do depart,
      Joys ebb and flow within my tender heart.

CHARLES BEST

My Love

There's not a fibre in my trembling frame
    That does not vibrate when thy step draws near,
    There's not a pulse that throbs not when I hear
Thy voice, thy breathing, nay thy very name.
    When thou art with me every sense seems dim,
    And all I am, or know, or feel is thee;
My soul grows faint, my veins run liquid flame,
    And my bewildered spirit seems to swim
    In eddying whirls of passion, dizzily.

When thou art gone, there creeps into my heart
     A cold and bitter consciousness of pain:
The light, the warmth of life with thee depart,
     And I sit dreaming over and over again
Thy greeting clasp, thy parting look and tone;
And suddenly I wake – and I am alone.

FANNY KEMBLE

Absence

Is Celadon unkind? it cannot be!
     Or is he so inconstant grown
     To slight my vows, and break his own?
Forbid it heaven! no, it cannot be!
Then, my good angel, whither is he fled?
Tell me – oh! tell me softly; is he dead?
     Ah! prophetic soul forbear!
     Lest I languish in despair;
No! my heart, when e'er he dies,
In the pain must sympathise:
Since my soul, and his are one,
He cannot live, or die, alone.
Florella, forbear to distrust, or repine,
Since his love, and his sufferings are equal with thine!
And when he returns, if ever again,
We'll laugh away sorrow, and kiss away pain.

ANONYMOUS

Remembrance

If grief for grief can touch thee,
If answering woe for woe,
If any ruth can melt thee,
Come to me now!

I cannot be more lonely,
More drear I cannot be!
My worn heart throbs so wildly
'Twill break for thee.

And when the world despises,
When heaven repels my prayer,
Will not mine angel comfort?
Mine idol hear?

Yes, by the tears I've poured thee,
By all my hours of pain,
O I shall surely win thee,
Beloved, again!

EMILY BRONTË

To Mary

I sleep with thee, and wake with thee,
    And yet thou art not there;
I fill my arms with thoughts of thee,
    And press the common air.
Thy eyes are gazing upon mine,
    When thou art out of sight;
My lips are always touching thine,
    At morning, noon, and night.

I think and speak of other things
    To keep my mind at rest:
But still to thee my memory clings
    Like love in woman's breast.
I hide it from the world's wide eye,
    And think and speak contrary;
But soft the wind comes from the sky,
    And whispers tales of Mary.

The night wind whispers in my ear,
    The moon shines in my face;
A burden still of chilling fear
    I find in every place.
The breeze is whispering in the bush,
    And the dews fall from the tree,
All sighing on, and will not hush,
    Some pleasant tales of thee.

JOHN CLARE

Every Moment I'm From Thy Sight

– Every moment
I'm from thy sight, the heart within my bosom
Moans like a tender infant in its cradle,
Whose nurse had left it.

THOMAS OTWAY

A Letter To Her Husband, Absent Upon Public Employment

As loving hind that (hartless) wants her deer,
Scuds through the woods and fern with hark'ning ear,
Perplexed, in every bush and nook doth pry
Her dearest deer might answer ear or eye:
So doth my anxious soul, which now doth miss
A dearer dear (far dearer heart) than this,
Still wait with doubts, and hopes, and failing eye,
His voice to hear or person to discry,
Or as the pensive dove doth all alone
On withered bough most uncouthly bemoan
The absence of her love and loving mate,
Whose loss hath made her so unfortunate:
Ev'n thus do I, with many a deep sad groan,
    Bewail my turtle true, who now is gone,

His presence and his safe return still woo
With thousand doleful sighs and mournful coo.
Or as the loving mullet, that true fish
Her fellow lost, nor joy nor life doth wish,
But lanches on that shore, there for to die
Where she her captive husband doth espy.
Mine being gone, I lead a joyless life,
I have a loving fere*, yet seem no wife:
But worst of all, to him can't steer my course,
I here, he there, alas, both kept by force.
Return my dear, my joy, my only love,
Unto thy hind, thy mullet and thy dove,
Who neither joys in pasture, house nor streams:
The substance gone, O me, these are but dreams.
Together at one tree, oh let us browse,
And like two turtles roost within one house,
And like the mullets in one river glide,
Let's still remain but one, till death divide.
    Thy loving love and dearest Dear,
      At home, abroad, and everywhere.

ANNE BRADSTREET

*companion

The Woods Are Still

The woods are still that were so gay at primrose-springing,
Through the dry woods the brown field-fares are winging,
And I alone of love, of love am singing.

I sing of love to the haggard palmer-worm,
Of love 'mid the crumpled oak-leaves that once were firm,
Laughing, I sing of love at the summer's term.

Of love, on a path where the snake's cast skin is lying,
Blue feathers on the floor, and no cuckoo flying;
I sing to the echo of my own voice crying.

MICHAEL FIELD

Psyche, Or The Legend Of Love

(EXTRACT)

There as she sought repose, her sorrowing heart
Recalled her absent love with bitter sighs;
Regret had deeply fixed the poisoned dart,
Which ever rankling in her bosom lies.

MARY TIGHE

Life Hangs Upon Me

– In my Lucia's absence
Life hangs upon me, and becomes a burden;
I am ten times more undone, while hope and fear,
And grief and rage, and love rise up at once,
And with variety of pain distract me.

JOSEPH ADDISON

A Pause

They made the chamber sweet with flowers and leaves
And the bed sweet with flowers on which I lay;
While my soul, love-bound, loitered on its way,
I did not hear the birds about the eaves,
Nor hear the reapers talk among the sheaves;
Only my soul kept watch from day to day,
My thirsty soul kept watch for one away;
Perhaps he loves, I thought, remembers, grieves.
At length there came the step upon the stair,
Upon the lock the old familiar hand:
Then first my spirit seemed to scent the air
Of paradise: then first the tardy sand
Of time ran golden, and I felt my hair
Put on a glory, and my soul expand.

CHRISTINA ROSSETTI

JEALOUSY

This Cursèd Jealousy

From THE SIEGE OF RHODES

This cursèd jealousy, what is't?
'Tis love that has lost itself in a mist;
'Tis love being frighted out his wits;
'Tis love that has a fever got;
Love that is violently hot,
But troubled with cold and trembling fits.
'Tis yet a more unnatural evil:
'Tis the god of love . . . possessed with a devil.
'Tis rich corrupted wine of love,
Which sharpest vinegar does prove;
From all the sweet flowers which might honey make,
It does a deadly poison bring:
Strange serpent which itself doth sting! . . .

SIR WILLIAM DAVENANT

She Charged Me

She charged me with having said this and that
To another woman long years before,
In the very parlour where we sat, –

Sat on a night when the endless pour
Of rain on the roof and the road below
Bent the spring of the spirit more and more . . .

– So charged she me; and the Cupid's bow
Of her mouth was hard, and her eyes, and her face,
And her white forefinger lifted slow.

Had she done it gently, or shown a trace
That not too curiously would she view
A folly flown ere her reign had place,

A kiss might have closed it. But I knew
From the fall of each word, and the pause between,
That the curtain would drop upon us two
Ere long, in our play of slave and queen.

THOMAS HARDY

Philanderer

In vain, dear Chloe, you suggest
That I, inconstant, have possessed
    Or loved a fairer she:
Would you with ease at once be cured
Of all the ills you've long endured,
    Consult your glass and me.

If then you think that I can find
A nymph more fair, or one more kind,
    You've reason for your fears:
But if impartial you will prove
To your own beauty and my love,
    How needless are your tears!

If, in my way, I should by chance
Receive, or give, a wanton glance
    I like but while I view;
How slight the glance, how faint the kiss,
Compared to that substantial bliss
    Which I receive from you!

With wanton flight the curious bee
From flower to flower still wanders free,
    And, where each blossom blows,
Extracts the juice of all he meets,
But for his quintessence of sweets
    He ravishes the rose.

So, my fond fancy to employ
On each variety of joy
    From nymph to nymph I roam;
Perhaps see fifty in a day;
Those are but visits which I pay –
    For Chloe is my home!

SIR WILLIAM YONGE

Love's Infiniteness

If yet I have not all thy love,
Dear, I shall never have it all,
I cannot breathe one other sigh, to move,
Nor can entreat one other tear to fall,
And all my treasure, which should purchase thee,
Sighs, tears, and oaths, and letters I have spent.
Yet no more can be due to me,
Than at the bargain made was meant,
If then thy gift of love were partial,
That some to me, some should to others fall,
    Dear, I shall never have thee all.

Or if then thou gavest me all,
All was but all, which thou hadst then;
But if in thy heart, since, there be or shall,
New love created be, by other men,
Which have their stocks entire, and can in tears,
In sighs, in oaths, and letter outbid me.
This new love may beget new fears,
For, this love was not vowed by thee,
And yet it was, thy gift being general,
The ground, thy heart is mine, what ever shall
    Grow there, dear, I should have it all.

Yet I would not have all yet,
He that hath all can have no more,
And since my love doth every day admit
New growth, thou shouldst have new rewards in store;
Thou canst not every day give me thy heart,
If thou canst give it, then thou never gavest it:
Love's riddles are, that though thy heart depart,
It stays at home, and thou with losing savest it:
But we will have a way more liberal,
Than changing hearts, to join them, so we shall
    Be one, and one another's all.

JOHN DONNE

Jealousy

'The myrtle bush grew shady
Down by the ford.'
'Is it even so?' said my lady.
'Even so!' said my lord.
'The leaves are set too thick together
For the point of a sword.

'The arras in your room hangs close,
No light between!
You wedded one of those that see unseen.'
'Is it even so?' said the King's Majesty.
'Even so!' said the Queen.

MARY COLERIDGE

Is Whispering Nothing?

From A WINTER'S TALE

Is whispering nothing?
Is leaning cheek to cheek? is meeting noses?
Kissing with inside lip? stopping the career
Of laughter with a sigh? (a note infallible
Of breaking honesty;) horsing foot on foot?
Skulking in corners? wishing clocks more swift?
Hours, minutes? noon, midnight? and all eyes
Blind with the pin and web, but theirs, theirs only,
That would, unseen, be wicked? – is this nothing?
Why, then the world and all that's in 't
The covering sky is nothing; Bohemia nothing,
My wife is nothing; nor nothing have these nothings,
If this be nothing.

WILLIAM SHAKESPEARE

Song

You wrong me, Strephon, when you say,
I'm jealous or severe,
Did I not see you kiss and play
With all you came a near?
Say, did I ever chide for this,
Or cast one jealous eye
On the bold nymphs, that snatched my bliss
While I stood willing by?

Yet though I never disapproved
This modish liberty;
I thought in them you only loved
Change and variety:
I vainly thought my charms so strong
And you so much my slave,
No nymph had power to do me wrong,
Or break the chains I gave.

But when you seriously address
With all your winning charms,
Unto a servile shepherdess,
I'll throw you from my arms:
I'd rather choose you should make love
To every face you see,
Than Mopsa's dull admirer prove
And let her rival me.

'EPHELIA'

Love's Sickness

Wretched and foolish jealousy
How cam'st thou thus to enter me?
    I ne'er was of thy kind:
Nor have I yet the narrow mind
    To vent that poor desire,
That others should not warm them at my fire:
    I wish the sun should shine
On all men's fruits and flowers as well as mine.

But under the disguise of love,
Thou say'st thou only cam'st to prove
    What my affections were.
Think'st thou that love is helped by fear?
    Go, get thee quickly forth,
Love's sickness and his noted want of worth,
    Seek doubting men to please.
I ne'er will owe my health to a disease.

BEN JONSON

O, Beware

From OTHELLO

O, beware, my lord, of jealousy;
It is the green-eyed monster which doth mock
The meat it feeds on: that cuckold lives in bliss
Who, certain of his fate, loves not his wronger;
But, O, what damned minutes tells he o'er
Who dotes, yet doubts, suspects, yet strongly loves!

WILLIAM SHAKESPEARE

My Pretty Rose Tree

A flower was offered to me,
Such a flower as May never bore;
But I said 'I've a pretty rose-tree,'
And I passed the sweet flower o'er.

Then I went to my pretty rose-tree,
To tend her by day and by night;
But my rose turned away with jealousy,
And her thorns were my only delight.

WILLIAM BLAKE

Grasped Too Close

I, whose life
Was bound with thine, by striving to secure
Thy beauties all my own, have killed the dove
I fondly grasped too close.

ELIJAH FENTON

He Who Binds Himself

He who binds himself to a joy
Does the wingèd life destroy;
But he who kisses the joy as it flies
Lives in eternity's sun rise.

WILLIAM BLAKE

Jealousy

O jealousy! Daughter of envy and love,
Most wayward issue of a gentle sire;
Fostered with fears, thy father's joys t' improve;
Mirth-marring monster, born a subtle liar;
Hateful unto thyself, flying thine own desire;
    Feeding upon suspect, that doth renew thee;
    Happy were lovers if they never knew thee.

Thou hast a thousand gates thou enterest by,
Condemning trembling passions to our heart:
Hundred-eyed Argus, ever-waking spy,
Pale hag, infernal fury, pleasure's smart,
Envious observer, prying in every part:
    Suspicious, fearful, gazing still about thee;
    O would to God that love could be without thee!

SAMUEL DANIEL

Merry Monarch

I pass all my hours in a shady old grove,
And I live not the day that I see not my love.
I survey every walk now my Phyllis is gone,
And sigh when I think we were there all alone.
    Oh, then 'tis! oh, then I think there's no such hell
    Like loving, like loving too well!

But each shade and each conscious bower when I find,
Where I once have been happy and she has been kind,
And I see the print left of her shape in the green,
And imagine the pleasure may yet come again;
    Oh, then 'tis! oh, then I think no joy's above
    The pleasures, the pleasures of love!

While alone to myself I repeat all her charms,
She I love may be locked in another man's arms:
She may laugh at my cares, and so false she may be
To say all the kind things she before said to me.
    Oh, then 'tis! oh, then I think there's no such hell
    Like loving, like loving too well!

But when I consider the truth of her heart,
Such an innocent passion, so kind, without art,
I fear I have wronged her, and hope she may be
So full of true love to be jealous of me.
    Oh, then 'tis! oh, then I think no joy's above
    The pleasures, the pleasures of love!

                        CHARLES II

To His Mistress

(EXTRACT)

My dear and only love, I pray
    This noble world of thee,
Be governed by no other sway
    But purest monarchy.
For if confusion have a part,
    Which virtuous souls abhor,
And hold a synod in thy heart,
    I'll never love thee more.

Like Alexander I will reign,
   And I will reign alone,
My thoughts shall evermore disdain
   A rival on my throne.
He either fears his fate too much,
   Or his deserts are small,
That puts it not unto the touch,
   To win or lose it all.

JAMES GRAHAM, MARQUIS OF MONTROSE

On Jealousy

O shield me from his rage, celestial powers!
This tyrant that embitters all my hours.
Ah, love! you've poorly played the hero's part,
You conquered, but you can't defend my heart.
When first I bent beneath your gentle reign,
I thought this monster banished from your train:
But you would raise him to support your throne,
And now he claims your empire as his own;
Or tell me, tyrants, have you both agreed
That where one reigns, the other shall succeed?

ESTHER JOHNSON

Love And Jealousy

How much are they deceived who vainly strive,
By jealous fears, to keep our flames alive?
Love's like a torch, which, if secured from blasts,
Will faintlier burn; but then it longer lasts.
Exposed to storms of jealousy and doubt,
The blaze grows greater, but 'tis sooner out.

WILLIAM WALSH

The Wrecks Of Wretched Men
From MITHRIDATES

Oh, my hard fate! Why did I trust her ever?
What story is not full of woman's falsehood?
The sex is all a sea of wide destruction:
We are vent'rous barks, that leave our home
For those sure dangers which their smiles conceal:
At first they draw us in with flatt'ring looks
Of summer calms, and a soft gale of sighs:
Sometimes, like sirens, charm us with their songs,
Dance on the waves, and show their golden locks;
But when the tempest comes, then, they leave us!
Or rather help the new calamity!
And the whole storm is one injurious woman!
The lightning followed with a thunderbolt,
Is marble-hearted woman! All the shelves,
The faithless winds, blind rocks, and sinking sands
Are woman all! the wrecks of wretched men!

NATHANIEL LEE

A Song

Strephon, your breach of faith and trust
    Affords me no surprise;
A man who grateful was, or just,
    Might make my wonder rise.

That heart to you so fondly tied,
    With pleasure wore its chain,
But from your cold neglectful pride,
    Found liberty again.

For this no wrath inflames my mind,
   My thanks are due to thee;
Such thanks as gen'rous victors find,
   Who set their captives free.

               LAETITIA PILKINGTON

Song

Foolish eyes, thy streams give over,
Wine, not water, binds the lover,
At the table then be shining.
Gay coquet, and all designing.
To th'addressing foplings bowing,
And thy smile, or hand, allowing,
Whine no more thy sacred passion,
Out of nature, out of fashion.

Let him disappointed find thee
False as he, nor dream to bind thee.
While he breaks all tender measures,
Murdering love, and all its pleasures.
Shall a look or word deceive thee,
Which he once an age will give thee?
Oh! no more, no more, excuse him,
Like a dull deserter use him.

               MARTHA SANSOM

To My Inconstant Mistress

When thou, poor excommunicate
   From all the joys of love, shalt see
The full reward, and glorious fate,
   Which my strong faith shall purchase me,
Then curse thine own inconstancy.

A fairer hand than thine, shall cure
    That heart, which thy false oaths did wound;
And to my soul, a soul more pure
    Than thine, shall by love's hand be bound,
And both with equal glory crowned.

Then shalt thou weep, entreat, complain
    To love, as I did once to thee;
When all thy tears shall be as vain
    As mine were then, for thou shalt be
Damned for thy false apostasy.

                    THOMAS CAREW

To Alexis In Answer To His Poem Against Fruition

Since man with inconstancy was born,
To love the absent, and the present scorn
    Why do we deck, why do we dress
    For such short-lived happiness?
    Why do we put attraction on,
Since either way 'tis we must be undone?

    They fly if honour take our part,
    Our virtue drives 'em o'er the field.
    We love 'em by too much desert,
    And oh! they fly us if we yield.
Ye gods! is there no charm in all the fair
To fix this wild, this faithless wanderer?

                    APHRA BEHN

A Lover's State

(EXTRACT)

Men are unconstant, and delight to range,
Not to gain freedom, but their fetters change:
And, what a year ago they did with passion seek,
Grows troublesome, and nauseous in a week:
And the poor lady, newly taught to love,
With grief and horror, sees her man remove.
Wonder not then thou canst no pleasure see,
But know thou seek'st it, where it cannot be.
Who vainly seeks for joys in love as well,
Might quiet seek in courts, and ease in hell.

'EPHELIA'

The Art Of Coquetry

(EXTRACT)

First form your artful looks with studious care,
From mild to grave, from tender to severe.
Oft on the careless youth your glances dart,
A tender meaning let each glance impart.
Whene'er he meet your looks, with modest pride
And soft confusion turn your eyes aside,
Let a soft sigh steal out, as if by chance,
Than cautious turn, and steal another glance.
Caught by these arts, with pride and hope elate,
The destined victim rushes on his fate:
Pleased, his imagined victory pursues,
And the kind maid with soft attention views,
Contemplates now her shape, her air, her face,
And thinks each feature wears an added grace;
Till gratitude, which first his bosom proves,
By slow degrees sublimed, at length he loves.

'Tis harder still to fix than gain a heart;
What's won by beauty must be kept by art.
Too kind a treatment the blessed lover cloys,
And oft despair the growing flame destroys:
Sometimes with smiles receive him, sometimes tears,
And wisely balance both his hopes and fears.
Perhaps he mourns his ill-requited pains,
Condemns your sway, and strives to break his chains;
Behaves as if he now your scorn defied,
And thinks at least he shall alarm your pride:
But with indifference view the seeming change,
And let your eyes to seek new conquests range;
While his torn breast with jealous fury burns,
He hopes, despairs, adores and hates by turns;
With anguish now repents the weak deceit,
And powerful passion bears him to your feet.

CHARLOTTE LENNOX

O Mighty Charm!

Trust not the treason of those smiling looks,
Until ye have their guileful trains well tried!
For they are like but unto golden hooks,
That from the foolish fish their baits do hide:
So she with flattering smiles weak hearts doth guide
Unto her love, and tempt to their decay;
Whom, being caught, she kills with cruel pride,
And feeds at pleasure on the wretched prey.
Yet even whilst her bloody hands them slay,
Her eyes look lovely, and upon them smile,
That they take pleasure in their cruel play,
And, dying, do themselves of pain beguile.
    O mighty charm! which makes men love their bane,
    And think they die with pleasure, live with pain.

EDMUND SPENSER

To His Forsaken Mistress

I do confess thou'rt smooth and fair,
    And I might have gone near to love thee,
Had I not found the slightest prayer
      That lips could move, had power to move thee;
        But I can let thee now alone,
        As worthy to be loved by none.

I do confess thou'rt sweet, yet find
    Thee such an unthrift of thy sweets,
Thy favours are but like the wind
      Which kisseth everything it meets;
        And since thou canst with more than one,
        Thou'rt worthy to be kissed by none.

The morning rose, that untouched stands
    Armed with her briars, how sweet she smells!
But plucked and strained through ruder hands,
      Her sweet no longer with her dwells,
        But scent and beauty both are gone,
        And leaves fall from her, one by one.

Such fate, ere long, will thee betide
    When thou has handled been a while,
With sere flowers to be thrown aside;
      And I shall sigh, when some will smile,
        To see thy love to every one
        Hath brought thee to be loved by none.

                          SIR ROBERT AYTON

Song

Nothing aids to love's fond fire
More than scorn and cold disdain
I to cherish your desire
Kindness used but 'twas in vain
You insulted on your slave

To be mine you soon refused.
Hope hope not then the power to have
Which ingloriously you used
Think not Thyrsis I will ere
By my love my empire loose
You grow constant through despair
Kindness you would soon abuse
Though you still possess my heart
Scorn and rigour I must fain
There remains no other art
Your love, fond fugitive, to gain.

ELIZABETH WILMOT

A Ballad Warning Men To Beware
Of Deceitful Women

(EXTRACT)

. . . Women, of kinde*, have conditions three;
The first is, that they be full of deceit;
To spin also it is their property;
And women have a wonderful conceit,
They wepen oft, and all is but a sleight,
And when they list, the tear is in the eye;
Beware therefore; the blind eat many a fly.

What thing than air is lighter and movable?
The leit†, men say, that passeth in a throw°;
Although the light be not so variable
As is the wind that every way can blow;
And yet, of reason, some men deem and trow
Women be lightest of their company;
Beware therefore; the blind eat many a fly.

In short to say, though all the earth so wan
Were parchëmente smooth white, and scribable,
And the great sea, cleped the ocean,
Were turned to inke, blacker than is sable,
Each stick a pen, each man a scrivener able,
They could not write woman's treachery;
Beware therefore; the blind eat many a fly.

JOHN LYDGATE

*by nature   †lightning   °instantly

Woman's Faith

Woman's faith, and woman's trust –
Write the characters in dust;
Stamp them on the running stream,
Print them on the moon's pale beam,
And each evanescent letter
Shall be clearer, firmer, better,
And more permanent, I ween,
Than the thing those letters mean.

I have strained the spider's thread
'Gainst the promise of a maid;
I have weighed a grain of sand
'Gainst her plight of heart and hand;
I told my true love of the token,
How her faith proved light, and her word was broken:
Again her word and truth she plight,
And I believed them again ere night.

SIR WALTER SCOTT

When Nettles In Winter Bring Forth Roses Red

When nettles in winter bring forth roses red,
   And all manner of thorn-trees bear figs naturally,
And geese bear pearls in every mead,
   And laurel bear cherries abundantly,
   And oaks bear dates very plenteously,
   And kisks give of honey superfluence,
   Then put women in trust and confidence . . .

When box bear paper in every land and town,
   And thistles bear berries in every place,
And pikes have naturally feathers in their crown,
   And bulls of the sea sing a good bass,
   And men by the ships fishes trace,
   And in women be found no insipience,
   Then put them in trust and confidence . . .

ANONYMOUS

Such False Soft Sighs

From MITHRIDATES

She has a tongue that can undo the world;
She eyes me just as when she first inflamed me:
Such were her looks, so melting was her language,
Such false soft sighs, and such deluding tears,
When from her lips I took the luscious poison,
When with that pleasing perjured breath avowing,
Her whispers trembled thro' my cred'lous ears,
And told the story of my utter ruin.

NATHANIEL LEE

Dione

(EXTRACT)

I will forgive, and (if I can)
Forget his wrongs to me,
His wrongs to me, who loved him long,
With matchless constancy.

Yet, are not all his sex alike?
Inconstant! false! unkind!
No vows, no promises of love,
Have power their hearts to bind.

The fault is ours, if, when they swear,
We foolishly believe,
But sure the greatest crime is theirs,
Who practise, to deceive.

SOPHIA BURRELL

An Answer To A Love-Letter

Is it to me, this sad lamenting strain?
Are heaven's choicest gifts bestowed in vain?
A plenteous fortune, and a beauteous bride,
Your love rewarded, gratified your pride:
Yet leaving her – 'tis me that you pursue
Without one single charm, but being new.
How vile is man! how I detest their ways
Of artful falsehood, and designing praise!
Tasteless, an easy happiness you slight,
Ruin your joy, and mischief your delight.
Why should poor pug (the mimic of your kind)
Wear a rough chain, and be to box confined?
Some cup, perhaps, he breaks, or tears a fan, –
While roves unpunished the destroyer, man.
Not bound by vows, and unrestrained by shame,
In sport you break the heart, and rend the fame.

Not that your art can be successful here,
Th'already plundered need no robber fear:
Nor sighs, nor charms, nor flatteries can move,
Too well secured against a second love.
Once, and but once, that devil charmed my mind;
To reason deaf, to observation blind;
I idly hoped (what cannot love persuade!)
My fondness equalled, and my love repaid;
Slow to distrust, and willing to believe,
Long hushed my doubts, and did myself deceive:
But oh! too soon – this tale would ever last;
Sleep, sleep my wrongs, and let me think 'em past.
For you who mourn with counterfeited grief,
And ask so boldly like a begging thief,
May soon some other nymph inflict the pain,
You know so well with cruel art to feign.
Tho' long you sported have with Cupid's dart;
You may see eyes, and you may feel a heart.
So the brisk wits, who stop the evening coach,
Laugh at the fear which follows their approach;
With idle mirth, and haughty scorn despise
The passenger's pale cheek, and staring eyes:
But seized by justice, find a fright no jest,
And all the terror doubled in their breast.

LADY MARY WORTLEY MONTAGU

The Forsaken Wife

Methinks, 'tis strange you can't afford
One pitying look, one parting word;
Humanity claims this as due,
But what's humanity to you?

    Cruel man! I am not blind,
Your infidelity I find;
Your want of love, my ruin shows,
My broken heart, your broken vows.
Yet maugre all your rigid hate,

I will be true in spite of fate;
And one pre-eminence I'll claim,
To be for ever still the same.

    Show me a man that dare be true.
That dares to suffer what I do;
That can for ever sigh unheard,
And ever love without regard:
I then will own your prior claim
To love, to honour, and to fame:
But 'till that time, my dear, adieu,
I yet superior am to you.

ELIZABETH THOMAS

Never Give All The Heart

Never give all the heart, for love
Will hardly seem worth thinking of
To passionate women if it seem
Certain, and they never dream
That it fades out from kiss to kiss;
For everything that's lovely is
But a brief, dreamy, kind delight.
O never give the heart outright,
For they, for all smooth lips can say,
Have given their hearts up to the play.
And who could play it well enough
If deaf and dumb and blind with love?
He that made this knows all the cost,
For he gave all his heart and lost.

W.B. YEATS

THE PAIN OF LOVE

Song

Love, a child, is ever crying;
Please him, and he straight is flying;
Give him, he the more is craving.
Never satisfied with having.

His desires have no measure;
Endless folly is his treasure;
What he promiseth he breaketh;
Trust not one word that he speaketh.

He vows nothing but false matter;
And to cozen you will flatter;
Let him gain the hand, he'll leave you,
And still glory to deceive you.

He will triumph in your wailing;
And yet cause be of your failing:
These his virtues are, and slighter
Are his gifts, his favours lighter.

Fathers are as firm in staying;
Wolves no fiercer in their preying:
As a child, then, leave him crying;
Nor seek him so given to flying.

LADY MARY WROTH

Love's Pains

This love, I canna' bear it,
It cheats me night and day;
This love, I canna' wear it,
It takes my peace away.

This love, wa' once a flower;
But now it is a thorn, –
The joy o' evening hour,
Turned to a pain ere morn.

This love, it wa' a bud,
And a secret known to me;
Like a flower within a wood;
Like a nest within a tree.

This love, wrong understood,
Oft turned my joy to pain;
I tried to throw away the bud,
But the blossom would remain.

JOHN CLARE

Song By Appelles

From CAMPASPE

Cupid and my Campaspe played
At cards for kisses, Cupid paid;
He stakes his quiver, bow and arrows,
His mother's doves, and team of sparrows;
Loses them too; then, down he throws
The coral of his lip, the rose
Growing on's cheek (but none knows how),
With these, the crystal of his brow,
And then the dimple of his chin:
All these did my Campaspe win.
At last, he set her both his eyes;
She won, and Cupid blind did rise.
    O love! has she done this to thee?
    What shall (alas!) become of me?

JOHN LYLY

Accursed Be Love

Accursed be love and they that trust his trains;
He tastes the fruit, whilst others toil:
He brings the lamp, we lend the oil:
He sows distress, we yield him soil:
He wageth war, we bide the foil:

Accursed be love, and those that trust his trains:
He lays the trap, we seek the snare:
He threat'neth death, we speak him fair:
He coins deceits, we foster care:
He favoureth pride, we count it rare.

THOMAS LODGE

Rosalind's Madrigal

Love in my bosom like a bee
   Doth suck his sweet;
Now with his wings he plays with me,
   Now with his feet.
Within mine eyes he makes his nest,
His bed amidst my tender breast;
My kisses are his daily feast,
And yet he robs me of my rest.
   Ah, wanton, will ye?

And if I sleep, then percheth he
   With pretty flight,
And makes his pillow of my knee
   The livelong night.
Strike I my lute, he tunes the string;
He music plays if so I sing;
He lends me every lovely thing;
Yet cruel he my heart doth sting.
   Whist, wanton, still ye!

Else I with roses every day
  Will whip you hence,
And bind you, when you long to play,
  For your offence.
I'll shut mine eyes to keep you in,
I'll make you fast it for your sin,
I'll count your power not worth a pin.
Alas! what hereby shall I win
  If he gainsay me?

What if I beat the wanton boy
  With many a rod?
He will repay me with annoy,
  Because a god.
Then sit thou safely.

THOMAS LODGE

The Garden Of Love

I went to the garden of love,
And saw what I never had seen:
A chapel was built in the midst,
Where I used to play on the green.

And the gates of this chapel were shut,
And 'Thou shalt not' writ over the door;
So I turned to the garden of love
That so many sweet flowers bore;

And I saw it was filled with graves,
And tomb-stones where flowers should be;
And priests in black gowns were walking their
  rounds,
And binding with briars my joys and desires.

WILLIAM BLAKE

A Prayer For Indifference

(EXTRACT)

I ask no kind return of love,
    No tempting charm to please;
Far from the heart those gifts remove,
    That sighs for peace and ease;

Nor peace, nor ease, the heart can know,
    That, like the needle true,
Turns at the touch of joy or woe,
    But, turning, trembles too.

Far as distress the soul can wound,
    'Tis pain in each degree:
'Tis bliss but to a certain bound,
    Beyond is agony.

FRANCES GREVILLE

O Curlew, Cry No More In The Air

O curlew, cry no more in the air.
Or only to the waters in the West;
Because your crying brings to mind
Passion-dimmed eyes and long heavy hair
That was shaken out over my breast:
There is enough evil in the crying of the wind.

Pale brows, still hands and dim hair
I had a beautiful friend
And dreamed that the old despair
Would end in love in the end:
She looked into my heart one day
And saw your image was there;
She has gone weeping away.

W.B. YEATS

The Clod And The Pebble

'Love seeketh not itself to please,
Nor for itself hath any care,
But for another gives its ease,
And builds a heaven in hell's despair.'

So sung a little clod of clay,
Trodden with the cattle's feet,
But a pebble of the brook
Warbled out these metres meet:

'Love seeketh only self to please,
To bind another to its delight,
Joys in another's loss of ease,
And builds a hell in heaven's despite.'

WILLIAM BLAKE

The Primrose

Ask me why I send you here,
This firstling of the infant year;
Ask me why I send to you,
This primrose all bepearled with dew;
I straight will whisper in your ears,
The sweets of love are washed with tears.

Ask me why this flower doth shew
So yellow, green, and sickly too;
Ask me why the stalk is weak,
And bending yet it doth not break;
I must tell you these discover,
What doubts and fears are in a lover.

THOMAS CAREW

Description Of Spring

WHEREIN EACH THING RENEWS,
SAVE ONLY THE LOVER

The sootë* season that bud and bloom forth brings,
With green hath clad the hill and eke the vale,
The nightingale with feathers new she sings;
The turtle to her mate hath told her tale:
Summer is come, for every spray now springs;
The hart hath hung his old head on the pale,
The buck in brake his winter coat he flings:
The fishes fleet with new repaired scale;
The adder all her slough away she flings;
The swift swallow pursueth the flies smale†,
The busy bee her honey now she mings°;
Winter is worn that was the flower's bale;
And thus I see among these pleasant things
Each care decays, and yet my sorrow springs.

HENRY HOWARD, EARL OF SURREY

*sweet   †small   °mingles

Modern Love

(EXTRACT)

Thus piteously love closed what he begat:
The union of this ever-diverse pair!
These two were rapid falcons in a snare,
Condemned to do the flitting of the bat.
Lovers beneath the singing sky of May,
They wandered once; clear as the dew on flowers.
But they fed not on the advancing hours:
Their hearts held cravings for the buried day.
Then each applied to each that fatal knife,
Deep questioning, which probes to endless dole,
Ah, what a dusty answer gets the soul
When hot for certainties in this our life! —

In tragic hints here see what evermore
Moves dark as yonder midnight ocean's force
Thundering like ramping hosts of warrior horse,
To throw that faint thin line upon the shore!

GEORGE MEREDITH

A Superscription

Look in my face; my name is Might-have-been;
    I am also called No-more, Too-late, Farewell;
    Unto thine ear I hold the dead-sea shell
Cast up thy life's foam-fretted feet between;
Unto thine eyes the glass where that is seen
    Which had life's form and love's, but by my spell
    Is now a shaken shadow intolerable,
Of ultimate things unuttered the frail screen.

Mark me, how still I am! But should there dart
    One moment through thy soul the soft surprise
    Of that winged peace which lulls the breath of sighs –
Then shalt thou see me smile, and turn apart
Thy visage to mine ambush at thy heart
    Sleepless with cold commemorative eyes.

DANTE GABRIEL ROSSETTI

Epilogue

Here lies a nymph! whose beauty was her bane,
Whose mind, in virtue's school, was taught in vain,
That outward charms acquire more excellence,
When ruled by chastity, and innocence:
She loved a youth, beyond her love of fame,
For him, disgraced the splendour of her name,
And when he ceased with partial eyes to view
Her charms, she gladly from the world withdrew . . .

May other nymphs, by her disgrace, forbear
To think their faces will continue fair,
Their lovers constant, or their friends sincere!
Beauty is doomed to be of transient date,
And love is oft the harbinger of hate,
At best, indifference coldly steps between,
Whilst sorrow calls on death to close the scene:
Then must the fading form lose all its grace,
And ev'ry blooming charm desert the face,
The broken heart shall rapidly decay,
And all the dreams of pleasure pass away,
The pulse shall cease to beat, the eye to weep,
And ev'ry trouble in the grave shall sleep . . .

SOPHIA BURRELL

Down By The Salley Gardens

Down by the salley gardens my love and I did meet;
She passed the salley gardens with little snow-white feet.
She bid me take love easy, as the leaves grow on the tree;
But I, being young and foolish, with her would not agree.

In a field by the river my love and I did stand,
And on my leaning shoulder she laid her snow-white hand.
She bid me take life easy, as the grass grows on the weirs;
But I was young and foolish, and now am full of tears.

W.B. YEATS

Consecration

Proud of my broken heart since thou didst break it,
    Proud of the pain I did not feel till thee,
Proud of my night since thou with moons dost slake it,
    Not to partake thy passion, my humility.

EMILY DICKINSON

The Way Of It

This is the way of it, wide world over,
One is beloved, and one is the lover,
    One gives and the other receives.
One lavishes all in a wild emotion,
One offers a smile for a life's devotion,
    One hopes and the other believes,
One lies awake in the night to weep,
And the other drifts off in a sweet sound sleep.

One soul is aflame with a godlike passion.
One plays with love in an idler's fashion,
    One speaks and the other hears.
One sobs, 'I love you,' and wet eyes show it,
And one laughs lightly, and says, 'I know it,'
    With smiles for the other's tears.
One lives for the other and nothing beside,
And the other remembers the world is wide.

This is the way of it, sad earth over,
The heart that breaks is the heart of the lover,
    And the other learns to forget.
'For what is the use of endless sorrow?
Though the sun goes down, it will rise tomorrow;
    And life is not over yet.'
Oh! I know this truth, if I know no other,
That passionate love is pain's own mother.

ELLA WHEELER WILCOX

Two Truths

'Darling,' he said, 'I never meant
    To hurt you;' and his eyes were wet.
'I would not hurt you for the world:
    Am I to blame if I forget?'

'Forgive my selfish tears!' she cried,
   'Forgive! I knew that it was not
Because you meant to hurt me, sweet –
   I knew it was that you forgot!'

But all the same, deep in her heart
   Rankled this thought, and rankles yet, –
'When love is at its best, one loves
   So much that he cannot forget.'

HELEN HUNT JACKSON

To Women, As Far As I'm Concerned

The feelings I don't have, I don't have.
The feelings I don't have, I won't say I have.
The feelings you say you have, you don't have.
The feelings you would like us both to have, we neither of
   us have.
The feelings people ought to have, they never have.
If people say they've got feelings, you may be
   pretty sure they
haven't got them.
So if you want either of us to feel anything at all
you'd better abandon all idea of feelings altogether.

D.H. LAWRENCE

The Bungler

You glow in my heart
Like the flames of uncounted candles.
But when I go to warm my hands,
My clumsiness overturns the light,
And then I stumble
Against the tables and chairs.

AMY LOWELL

Once We Played

Once we played at love together –
    Played it smartly, if you please;
Lightly, as a windblown feather,
    Did we stake a heart apiece.

Oh, it was delicious fooling!
    In the hottest of the game,
Without thought of future cooling,
    All too quickly burned life's flame.

In this give-and-take of glances,
    Kisses sweet as honey dews.
When we played with equal chances,
    Did you win, or did I lose?

MATHILDE BLIND

My Heart Was Slain

My heart was slain, and none but you and I;
Who should I think the murder should commit?
Since but yourself there was no creature by,
But only I; guiltless of murd'ring it.
It slew itself; the verdict on the view
Do quit the dead, and me not accessory:
Well, well, I fear it will be proved by you,
The evidence so great a proof doth carry.
But O, see, see, we need inquire no further,
Upon your lips the scarlet drops are found,
And in your eye the boy that did the murder,
Your cheeks yet pale, since first he gave the wound,
    By this I see, however things be past,
    Yet heaven will still have murder out at last.

MICHAEL DRAYTON

'Twere Better To Lose The Fire

Such love is like a smoky fire
In a cold morning. Though the fire be cheerful,
Yet is the smoke so foul and cumbersome,
'Twere better lose the fire, than find the smoke.

GEORGE CHAPMAN

Intimates

Don't you care for my love? she said bitterly.

I handed her the mirror, and said:
Please address these questions to the proper person!
Please make all request to head-quarters!
In all matters of emotional importance
please approach the supreme authority direct!
So I handed her the mirror.

And she would have broken it over my head,
but she caught sight of her own reflection
and that held her spellbound for two seconds
while I fled.

D.H. LAWRENCE

Gorgeous Covers Wall Up Filthy Books

Unless there were consent 'twixt hell and heaven
That grace and wickedness should be combined,
I cannot make thee and thy beauties even;
Thy face is heaven, and torture in thy mind;
For more than worldly bliss is in thy eye,
And hellish torture in thy mind doth lie.

A thousand cherubins fly in her looks,
And hearts in legions melt upon their view:
But gorgeous covers wall up filthy books;
Be it sin to say, that so your eyes do you:
But, sure, your mind adheres not with your eyes,
For what they promise, that your heart denies.

But, O, lest I religion should misuse,
Inspire me thou, that ought'st thy self to know,
Since skilless readers reading do abuse
What inward meaning outward sense doth show;
For by thy eyes and heart, chos'n and contemned,
I waver, whether savèd or condemned.

                                        THOMAS CAMPION

Song

O love is so deceiving
Like bees it wears a sting.
I thought it true believing
But it's no such thing.
They smile but to deceive you
They kiss and then they leave you
Speak truth they won't believe you
Their honey wears a sting.

What's the use o' pretty faces
Ruby lips and cheeks so red?
Flowers grow in pleasant places
So does a maidenhead.
The fairest won't believe you,
The foulest all deceive you,
The many laugh and grieve you
Until your coffin dead.

                                        JOHN CLARE

Sphinx

But why do I feel so strangely about you?
said the lovely young lady, half wistful, half menacing.

I took to my heels and ran
before she could set the claws of her self-conscious questioning in me
or tear me with the fangs of disappointment
because I could not answer the riddle of her own self-importance.

D.H. LAWRENCE

Carrefour

O you,
Who came upon me once
Stretched under apple-trees just after bathing,
Why did you not strangle me before speaking
Rather than fill me with the wild white honey of your words
And then leave me to the mercy
Of the forest bees?

AMY LOWELL

Vixi Puellis Nuper Idoneus . . .

They flee from me that sometime did me seek,
   With naked foot stalking within my chamber:
Once I have seen them gentle, tame, and meek,
   That now are wild, and do not once remember
   That sometime they have put themselves in danger
To take bread at my hand; and now they range,
Busily seeking in continual change.

Thankèd be fortune, it hath been otherwise
    Twenty times better; but once especial –
In thin array, after a pleasant guise,
    When her loose gown did from her shoulders fall,
    And she me caught in her arms long and small,
And therewithal so sweetly did me kiss,
And softly said, 'Dear heart, how like you this?'

It was no dream, for I lay broad awaking:
    But all is turned now, through my gentleness,
Into a bitter fashion of forsaking;
    And I have leave to go of her goodness;
    And she also to use new-fangledness.
But since that I unkindly so am served,
'How like you this?' – what hath she now deserved?

SIR THOMAS WYATT

Loving In Truth

Loving in truth, and fain in verse my love to show,
    That she, dear she, might take some pleasure of my pain,
Pleasure might cause her read, reading might make her know,
    Knowledge might pity win, and pity grace obtain,
I sought fit words to paint the blackest face of woe;
    Studying inventions fine, her wits to entertain,
Oft turning others' leaves to see if thence would flow
    Some fresh and fruitful showers upon my sun-burned brain.
But words came halting forth, wanting invention's stay;
    Invention, nature's child, fled step-dame study's blows,
And others' feet still seemed but strangers in my way.
    Thus, great with child to speak, and helpless in my throes,
        Biting my truant pen, beating myself for spite,
            'Fool,' said my muse to me, 'look in thy heart and write.'

SIR PHILIP SIDNEY

On Monsieur's Departure

I grieve and dare not show my discontent;
    I love, and yet am forced to seem to hate;
I do, yet dare not say I ever meant;
    I seem stark mute, but inwardly do prate:
I am, and not: I freeze, and yet am burned,
Since from myself, my other self I turned.

My care is like my shadow in the sun,
    Follows me flying, flies when I pursue it;
Stands and lies by me, does what I have done;
    This too familiar care does make me rue it:
No means I find to rid him from my breast,
Till by the end of things it be suppressed.

Some gentler passions slide into my mind,
    For I am soft, and made of melting snow;
Or be more cruel, love, and so be kind,
    Let me float or sink, be high or low:
Or let me live with some more sweet content,
Or die, and so forget what love e'er meant.

ELIZABETH I

My Love Is A Fever

My love is a fever, longing still
For that which longer nurseth the disease,
Feeding on that which doth preserve the ill,
The uncertain sickly appetite to please.
My reason, the physician to my love,
Angry that his prescriptions are not kept,
Hath left me, and I desperate now approve
Desire is death, which physic did except.
Past cure I am, now reason is past care,
And frantic-mad with evermore unrest;

My thoughts and my discourse as madmen's are,
At random from the truth vainly expressed.
    For I have sworn thee fair, and thought thee bright,
    Who art as black as hell, as dark as night.

WILLIAM SHAKESPEARE

To Lysander

(ON SOME VERSES HE WRIT, AND ASKING MORE FOR HIS HEART THAN IT WAS WORTH)

Take back the heart you with such caution give,
    Take the fond valued trifle back:
I hate love merchants that a trade would drive
    And meanly cunning bargains make.

I care not how the busy market goes
    And scorn to chaffer for a price:
Love does one staple rate on all impose,
    Nor leaves it to the trader's choice.

A heart requires a heart unfeigned and true,
    Though subtly you advance the price;
And ask a rate that simple love ne'er knew
    And the free trade monopolize.

An humble slave the buyer must become,
    She must not bate a look or glance
You will have all or you'll have none;
    See how love's market you enhance.

It's not enough I gave you heart for heart,
    But I must add my lips and eyes;
I must no smile or friendly kiss impart;
    But you must dun me with advice . . .

Be just, my lovely swain, and do not take
    Freedoms you'll not to me allow:
O give Aminta so much freedom back
    That she may rove as well as you.

Let us then love upon the honest square
   Since interest neither have designed,
For the sly gamester, who ne'er plays me fair
   Must trick for trick expect to find.

APHRA BEHN

Love's Consolation

(EXTRACT)

. . . Love hath great store of sweetness, and 'tis well;
A moment's heaven pays back an age of hell . . .
Yea, and to have seen
Thy lady walking in a garden green,
Mid apple blossoms and green twisted boughs,
Along the golden gravel path, to house
Herself, where thou art watching far below,
Deep in thy bower impervious, even though
Thou never give her kisses after that,
Is sweeter than to never break the flat
Of thy soul's rising, like a river tide
That never foams; yea, if thy lady chide
Cruelly thy service, and indeed becomes
A wretch, whose false eyes haunt thee in all rooms,
'Tis better so, than never to have been
An hour in love; than never to have seen
Thine own heart's worthiness to shrink and shake,
Like silver quick, all for thy lady's sake,
Weighty with truth, with gentleness as bright.
    Moreover, let sad lovers take delight
In this, that time will bring at last their peace:
We watch great passions in their huge increase,
Until they fill our hearts, so that we say,
'Let go this, and I die'; yet nay and nay,
We find them leave us strangely quiet then,
When they must quit; one lion leaves the den,
Another enters; wherefore thus I cross
All lovers pale and starving with their loss.

And yet, and yet, and yet, how long I tore
My heart, O love! how long, O love! before
I could endure to think of peace, and call
For remedy, from what time thou didst all
Shatter with one bad word, and bitter ruth
Didst mete me for thy patience and my truth . . .

RICHARD WATSON DIXON

Why?

Why did you come, with your enkindled eyes
And mountain-look, across my lower way.
And take the vague dishonour from my day
By luring me from paltry things, to rise
And stand beside you, waiting wistfully
The looming of a larger destiny?

Why did you with strong fingers fling aside
The gates of possibility, and say
With vital voice the words I dream to-day?
Before, I was not much unsatisfied:
But since a god has touched me and departed,
I run through every temple, broken-hearted.

MARY WEBB

For Love Can Be Tender At Morning

I have grown weary of loving, weary of love and its pain;
I would sing again in the sunshine, would laugh in the beating rain;
I would thank the grass for its greenness, and know joy in the light;
The dawn would show me its secrets, and the moon bless me
    by night.

For love can be tender at morning, and break your heart ere eve,
It can drug your soul with its sweetness, then shatter the dreams
   you weave.
Oh, love is as easily tarnished as the bloom in the heart of a rose,
And, swift as a sweet rose fadeth, yet swifter love's beauty goes. –

The soul of a rose still lingers, frail scent o'er its petals dead;
But the soul of a love that has vanished leaves only an ache in
   its stead.
For love can be tender at morning, and break your heart ere eve;
It can drug your soul with its sweetness – then shatter the dreams
   you weave.

MAIMIE A. RICHARDSON

Love's Eye The Jewel Of Sleep, Oh! Seldom Wears

From BLUNT, MASTER CONSTABLE

'Alas! how can I sleep? who truly loves,
Burns out the day in idle fantasies;
And when the lamb bleating doth bid goodnight
Unto the closing day, then tears begin
To keep quick time unto the owl, whose voice
Shrieks like the bellman in the lover's ears:
Love's eye the jewel of sleep, oh! seldom wears.

The early lark is wakened from her bed,
Being only in love's plaints disquieted;
And singing in the morning's ear she weeps,
Being deep in love, at lovers' broken sleeps.
But say a golden slumber chance to tie
With silken strings the cover of love's eye;
Then dreams, magician-like, mocking present
Pleasures, whose fading leaves more discontent.'

THOMAS MIDDLETON

Away Delights!

From THE CAPTAIN

Away, delights! go seek some other dwelling,
For I must die.
Farewell, false love! thy tongue is ever telling
Lie after lie,
For ever let me rest now from thy smarts;
Alas, for pity, go,
And fire their hearts
That have been hard to thee! Mine was not so . . .

JOHN FLETCHER

The Mermaid

A mermaid found a swimming lad,
Picked him for her own,
Pressed her body to his body,
Laughed; and plunging down
Forgot in cruel happiness
That even lovers drown.

W.B. YEATS

LOVE'S INTIMACY

A Ditty

My true-love hath my heart, and I have his,
By just exchange one to the other given:
I hold his dear, and mine he cannot miss,
There never was a better bargain driven:
    My true-love hath my heart, and I have his.

His heart in me keeps him and me in one,
My heart in him his thoughts and senses guides:
He loves my heart, for once it was his own,
I cherish his because in me it bides:
    My true-love hath my heart, and I have his.

SIR PHILIP SIDNEY

Transcendent Pleasure

How transcendent is the pleasure,
    Which congenial souls must know;
When each heart, in equal measure,
    Beats to bliss, or sinks to woe!

When with kindred feelings glowing,
    Tho' by various modes expressed;
Smiles unbid, or tears fast flowing
    Show alike the tender breast.

ANONYMOUS

Because We Two Must Never Part

Dear, let us two each other spy:
How curious! In each other's eye
We're drawn to life, and thus we see
Ourselves at once, both thee and me,
Distinctly two, yet not alone,
Incorporated, that's but one.

My picture in your eyes you bear:
I yours, as much as mine you wear.
'Tis not our spreties can not pass,
Or shining makes a looking glass,
Nor picture, really we lie
Contracted each in other's eye.

When that our milk-white purer lawn,
Our eyelid curtains, when they're drawn,
Soft sleep, made with sweet vapours' rain,
To cool us shrinks into each brain,
Rejoicing with love's running streams,
Which grosser lovers call but dreams.

Because we two must never part,
We move down to each other's heart,
And there, all passions turned to joy,
Our loving hearts feel no annoy
Delated, lest our souls outskips
With joy, kiss quickly! stop our lips!

WILLIAM CAVENDISH, DUKE OF NEWCASTLE

Love Song

There is a strong wall about me to protect me:
It is built of the words you have said to me.

There are swords about me to keep me safe:
They are the kisses of your lips.

Before me goes a shield to guard me from harm:
It is the shadow of your arms between me and danger.

All the wishes of my mind know your name,
And the white desires of my heart
They are acquainted with you.
The cry of my body for completeness,
That is a cry for you.
My blood beats out your name to me, unceasing, pitiless
Your name, your name.

MARY CAROLYN DAVIES

Two Made One

My end is lost in loving of a face,
An eye, lip, nose, hand, foot, or other part,
Whose all is but a statue, if the mind
Move not, which only can make the return.
The end of love is, to have two made one
In will, and in affection, that the minds
Be first innoculated, not the bodies.

BEN JONSON

I Would Live In Your Love

I would live in your love as the sea-grasses live in the sea,
Borne up by each wave as it passes, drawn down by each wave
    that recedes;
I would empty my soul of the dreams that have gathered in me,
I would beat with your heart as it beats, I would follow your soul
    as it leads.

SARA TEASDALE

To My Dearest Lucasia

The compasses that stand above
Express this great immortal love:
For friends, like them, can prove this true,
They are, and yet they are not, two.

And in their posture expressed
Friendship's exalted interest:
Each follows where the other leans,
And what each does, this other means.

And as when one foot does stand fast,
And t'other circles seeks to cast,
The steady part does regulate
And make the wanderer's motion straight:

So friends are only two in this,
T' reclaim each other when they miss:
For whosoe'er will grossly fall,
Can never be a friend at all . . .

KATHERINE PHILIPS

I Loved You First

Poco favilla gran fiamma seconda - DANTE
Ogni altra cos, ogni pensier va fore,
E sol ivi con voi rimansi amore. - PETRARCA

I loved you first: but afterwards your love
    Outsoaring mine, sang such a loftier song
As drowned the friendly cooings of my dove.
    Which owes the other most? my love was long,
    And yours one moment seemed to wax more strong;
I loved and guessed at you, you constructed me
And loved me for what might or might not be –
    Nay, weights and measures do us both a wrong.
For verily love knows not 'mine' or 'thine';

With separate 'I' and 'thou' free love has done,
    For one is both and both are one in love:
Rich love knows nought of thine that is not mine;
    Both have the strength and both the length thereof,
Both of us, of the love which makes us one.

CHRISTINA ROSSETTI

Go From Me

SONNET FROM THE PORTUGUESE VI

Go from me. Yet I feel that I shall stand
    Henceforward in thy shadow. Nevermore
    Alone upon the threshold of my door
Of individual life I shall command
The uses of my soul, nor lift my hand
    Serenely in the sunshine as before,
    Without the sense of that which I forbore –
Thy touch upon the palm. The widest land
Doom takes to part us, leaves thy heart in mine
    With pulses that beat double. What I do
And what I dream include thee, as the wine
    Must taste of its own grapes. And when I sue
God for myself, He hears that name of thine,
    And sees within my eyes the tears of two.

ELIZABETH BARRETT BROWNING

To Cynthia On Her Embraces

If thou a reason dost desire to know,
My dearest Cynthia, why I love thee so,
As when I do enjoy all thy love's store,
I am not yet content, but seek for more;
When we do kiss so often as the tale
Of kisses doth outvie the winter's hail:

When I do print them on more close and sweet
Than shells of scallops, cockles when they meet,
Yet am not satisfied: when I do close
Thee nearer to me than the ivy grows
Unto the oak: when those white arms of thine
Clip me more close than doth the elm the vine:
When naked both, thou seemest not to be
Contiguous, but continuous parts of me:
And we in bodies are together brought
So near, our souls may know each other's thought
Without a whisper: yet I do aspire
To come more close to thee, and to be higher.
No, 'twas well said, that spirits are too high
For bodies, when they meet, to satisfy;
Our souls having like forms of light and sense,
Proceeding from the same intelligence,
Desire to mix like to two water drops,
Whose union some little hindrance stops,
Which meeting both together would be one.
For in the steel, and in the adamant stone,
One and the same magnetic soul is cause,
That with such unseen chains each other draws:
So our souls now divided, brooked not well,
That being one, they should asunder dwell.
Then let me die, that so my soul being free,
May join with that her other half in thee,
For when in thy pure self it shall abide,
It shall assume a body glorified,
Being in that high bliss; nor shall we twain
Or wish to meet, or fear to part again.

SIR FRANCIS KYNASTON

Give Me Myself

You're not alone when you are still alone:
O God, from you that I could private be!
Since you one were, I never since was one,

Since you in me, my self since out of me.
Transported from myself into your being,
Though either distant, present yet to either;
Senseless with too much joy, each other seeing,
And only absent when we are together.
Give me my self, and take your self again!
Devise some means but how I may forsake you!
So much is mine that doth with you remain,
That taking what is mine, with me I take you.
    You do bewitch me! O that I could fly
    From my self you, or from your own self I!

MICHAEL DRAYTON

A Divine Rapture

E'en like two little bank-dividing brooks,
    That wash the pebbles with their wanton streams,
And having ranged and searched a thousand nooks,
    Meet both at length in silver-breasted Thames,
Where in a greater current they conjoin:
So I my best-belovèd's am; so he is mine.

E'en so we met; and after long pursuit,
    E'en so we joined; we both became entire;
No need for either to renew a suit,
    For I was flax and he was flames of fire:
Our firm-united souls did more than twine;
So I my best-belovèd's am; so he is mine.

If all those glittering monarchs that command
    The servile quarters of this earthly ball,
Should tender in exchange, their shares of land,
    I would not change my fortunes for them all:
Their wealth is but a counter to my coin:
The world's but theirs; but my belovèd's mine.

FRANCIS QUARLES

To Mrs Mary Awbrey

Soul of my soul, my joy, my crown, my friend,
A name which all the rest doth comprehend;
How happy are we now, whose souls are grown,
By an incomparable mixture, one:
Whose well-acquainted minds are now as near
As love, or vows, or friendship can endear?
I have no thought but what's to thee revealed,
Nor thou desire that is from me concealed.
Thy heart locks up my secrets richly set,
And my breast is thy private cabinet.
Thou shed'st no tear but what my moisture lent,
And if I sigh, it is thy breath is spent.
United thus, what horror can appear
Worthy our sorrow, anger, or our fear?
Let the dull world alone to talk and fight,
And with their vast ambitions nature fright;
Let them despise so innocent a flame,
While envy, pride, and faction play their game:
But we by love sublimed so high shall rise,
To pity kings, and conquerors despise,
Since we that sacred union have engrost,
Which they and all the factious world have lost.

KATHERINE PHILIPS

The Good-Morrow

I wonder, by my troth, what thou and I
Did, till we loved? were we not weaned till then?
But sucked on country pleasures, childishly?
Or snorted we in the Seven Sleepers' den?
'Twas so; but this, all pleasures fancies be;
If ever any beauty I did see,
Which I desired, and got, 'twas but a dream of thee.

And now good-morrow to our waking souls,
Which watch not one another out of fear;
For love all love of other sights controls,
And makes one little room an everywhere.
Let sea-discoverers to new worlds have gone;
Let maps to other, worlds on worlds have shown;
Let us possess one world; each hath one, and is one.

My face in thine eye, thine in mine appears,
And true plain hearts do in the faces rest;
Where can we find two better hemispheres
Without sharp north, without declining west;
Whatever dies was not mixed equally;
If our two loves be one, or thou and I
Love so alike that none can slacken, none can die.

JOHN DONNE

The Avenue

Who has not seen their lover
Walking at ease,
Walking like any other
A pavement under trees,
Not singular, apart,
But footed, featured, dressed,
Approaching like the rest
In the same dapple of the summer caught;
Who has not suddenly thought
With swift surprise:
There walks in cool disguise,
There comes, my heart.

FRANCES CORNFORD

Soft Love, Spontaneous Tree

Soft love, spontaneous tree, its parted root
Must from two hearts with equal vigour shoot;
Whilst each delighted and delighting gives
The pleasing ecstasy which each receives:
Cherished with hope, and fed with joy, it grows,
Its cheerful buds their op'ning bloom disclose
And round the happy soil diffusive odour flows.
If angry fate that mutual care denies,
The fading plant bewails its due supplies;
Wild with despair, or sick with grief, it dies.

MATTHEW PRIOR

Epitaph

His being was in her alone:
And he not being, she was none.

They joyed one joy, one grief they grieved;
One love they loved, one life they lived.
The hand was one, one was the sword,
That did his death, her death afford.

As all the rest, so now the stone
That tombs the two is justly one.

SIR PHILIP SIDNEY

Epitaph

These are two friends whose lives were undivided,
So let their memory be, now they have glided
Under the grave; let not their bones be parted
For their two hearts in life were single-hearted.

ANONYMOUS

MARRIAGE

Honest Wedlock

. . . I scent the air
Of blessings, when I come but near the house;
What a delicious breath marriage sends forth;
The violet bed's not sweeter! Honest wedlock
Is like a banqueting house, built in a garden,
On which the spring's chaste flowers take delight
To cast their modest odours; when base lust,
With all her powders, paintings, and best pride,
Is but a fair house built in a morass.

THOMAS MIDDLETON

To My Dear And Loving Husband

If ever two were one, then surely we.
If ever man were loved by wife, then thee.
If ever wife was happy in a man,
Compare with me, ye woman, if you can.
I prize thy love more than whole mines of gold,
Or all the riches that the east doth hold.
My love is such that rivers cannot quench,
Nor aught but love from thee give recompense.
Thy love is such I can no way repay;
The heavens reward thee manifold I pray.
Then while we live, in love let's so persèver,
That when we love no more, we may live ever.

ANNE BRADSTREET

My Wife

Trusty, dusky, vivid, true,
With eyes of gold and bramble-dew,
Steel-true and blade-straight,
The great artificer
Made my mate.

Honour, anger, valour, fire;
A love that life could never tire,
Death quench or evil stir,
The mighty master
Gave to her.

Teacher, tender, comrade, wife,
A fellow-farer true through life,
Heart-whole and soul-free
The august father
Gave to me.

ROBERT LOUIS STEVENSON

Love's Matrimony

There is no happy life
But in a wife;
The comforts are so sweet
When they do meet:
'Tis plenty, peace, a calm
Like dropping balm:
Love's weather is so fair,
Perfumèd air,
Each word such pleasure brings
Like soft-touched strings;
Love's passion moves the heart
On either part.

Such harmony together,
So pleased in either,
No discords, concords still,
Sealed with one will.
By love, God man made one,
Yet not alone:
Like stamps of king and queen
It may be seen,
Two figures but one coin;
So they do join,
Only they not embrace,
We face to face.

WILLIAM CAVENDISH, DUKE OF NEWCASTLE

Advice To Her Son On Marriage

When you gain her affection, take care to preserve it;
Lest others persuade her, you do not deserve it.
Still study to heighten the joys of her life;
Not treat her the worse, for her being your wife.
If in judgement she errs, set her right, without pride:
'Tis the province of insolent fools to deride.
A husband's first praise is a friend and protector:
Then change not these titles for tyrant and hector.
Let your person be neat, unaffectedly clean,
Tho' alone with your wife the whole day you remain.
Choose books for her study to fashion her mind,
To emulate those who excelled of her kind.
Be religion the principal care of your life,
As you hope to be blest in your children and wife;
So you, in your marriage, shall gain its true end;
And find, in your wife, a companion and friend.

MARY BARBER

A Wife's Conquest

Ye fair married dames, who so often deplore,
That a lover once blessed is a lover no more;
Attend to my counsel, nor blush to be taught,
That prudence must cherish what beauty has caught.

The bloom of your cheek, and the glance of your eye,
Your roses and lilies may make the men sigh;
But roses and lilies and sighs pass away,
And passion will die as your beauties decay.

Use the man that you wed, like your favourite guitar,
Though music's in both, they are both apt to jar;
How tuneful and soft from a delicate touch,
Not handled too roughly, nor played on too much.

The sparrow and linnet will feed from your hand,
Grow tame by your kindness and come at command:
Exert with your husband the same happy skill;
For hearts, like your birds, may be tamed to your will.

Be gay and good-humoured, complying and kind;
Turn the chief of your care, from your face to your mind;
'Tis there that a wife may her conquest improve,
And Hymen shall rivet the fetters of love.

DAVID GARRICK

O Donald! Ye Are Just The Man

O Donald! ye are just the man
    Who, when he's got a wife,
Begins to fratch — nae notice ta'en —
    They're strangers a' their life.

The fan may drop – she takes it up,
  The husband keeps his chair;
She hands the kettle – gives his cup –
  Without e'en – 'thank ye, dear.'

Now, truly, these slights are but toys;
  But frae neglects like these,
The wife may soon a slattern grow,
  And strive nae mair to please.

For wooers ay do all they can
  To trifle wi' the mind;
They hold the blaze of beauty up,
  And keep the poor things blind.

But wedlock tears away the veil,
  The goddess is nae mair;
He thinks his wife a silly thing,
  She thinks her man a bear.

Let then the lover be the friend –
  The loving friend for life;
Think but thysel' the happiest spouse,
  She'll be the happiest wife.

SUSANNA BLAMIRE

Good Husbands Make Unhappy Wives

Good husbands make unhappy wives
so do bad husbands, just as often;
but the unhappiness of a wife with a good husband
is much more devastating
than the unhappiness of a wife with a bad husband.

D.H. LAWRENCE

The Farmer's Bride

Three summers since I chose a maid,
Too young maybe – but more's to do
At harvest-time than bide and woo.
When us was wed she turned afraid
Of love and me and all things human;
Like the shut of a winter's day
Her smile went out, and 'twadn't a woman –
More like a little frightened fay.
One night, in the fall, she runned away.

'Out 'mong the sheep, her be,' they said,
Should properly have been abed;
But sure enough she wadn't there
Lying awake with her wide brown stare.
So over seven-acre field and up-along across the down
We chased her, flying like a hare
Before our lanterns. To Church-Town
All in a shiver and a scare
We caught her, fetched her home at last
And turned the key upon her, fast.

She does the work about the house
As well as most, but like a mouse:
Happy enough to cheat and play
With birds and rabbits and such as they,
So long as men-folk keep away
'Not near, not near!' her eyes beseech
When one of us comes within reach.
The women say that beasts in stall
Look round like children at her call.
I've hardly heard her speak at all.
Shy as a leveret, swift as he,
Straight and slight as a young larch tree,
Sweet as the first wild violets, she,
To her wild self. But what to me?

The short days shorten and the oaks are brown,
The blue smoke rises to the low grey sky,
One leaf in the still air falls slowly down,
A magpie's spotted feathers lie
On the black earth spread white with rime,
The berries redden up to Christmas-time.
What's Christmas-time without there be
Some other in the house than we!

She sleeps up in the attic there
Alone, poor maid. 'Tis but a stair
Betwixt us. Oh! my God! the down,
The soft young down of her, the brown,
The brown of her – her eyes, her hair, her hair!

CHARLOTTE MEW

Letter To Miss E.B. On Marriage

(EXTRACT)

Mankind should hope, in wedlock's state,
A friend to find as well as mate:
And ere the charm of person fails,
Enquire what merit there remains,
That may, by help of their wise pate,
Be taught through life to bless the state;
And oft they'd find, by their own fire,
What they in others so admire.
But as 'tis law that each good wife
Should true submission show for life,
What's right at home they often slight,
What's right abroad shines very bright.

Each female would have regal power,
But every male wants something more;
And that same balsam to the mind,
Which both would in compliance find,
Is, to this very time and hour,
Miscalled by them the want of power.
Then right of privilege they claim,
For every fair to vow a flame,
Which we are bound, with partial eye,
To find of true platonic dye;
For they've so fixed the certain rule,
How far with ladies they may fool,
That 'tis impossible they can
Go wrong – though not a man
Among them all would patience find,
If lady-wife should be inclined
To praise each swain, whose face or wit
Might chance her sprightly mind to hit.

Then there's something in the mind,
That is not only just – but kind;
That's fixed to neither taste nor sense,
Nor to be taught by eloquence;
But yet is that which gives a grace
To every feature of the face;
And is the surest chance for ease:
I mean a strong desire to please.
But own I must (though 'tis with shame)
Both parties are in this to blame;
They take great pains to come together,
Then squabble for a straw or feather;
And oft I fear a spark of pride
Prevails too much on either side.

Then hear, my girl – if 'tis your lot
To marry, be not this forgot:
That neither sex must think to find
Perfection in the human kind;
Each has a fool's cap – and a bell –
And, what is worse, can't always tell
(While they have got it on their head)

How far astray they may be led.
Let it be then your mutual care,
That never both at once may wear
This fatal mark of reason's loss,
That whirlwind-like the soul does toss.
Obtain this point, and friendship's power
Will rise and bless each future hour.

MARY SAVAGE

On An Hour-Glass

(EXTRACT)

. . . This gapes for marriage, yet his fickle head
Knows not what cares wait on the marriage bed:
This vows virginity, yet knows not what
Loneness, grief, discontent, attend that state . . .

JOHN HALL

Prudent Marriage

Let reason teach what passion fain would hide,
That Hymen's bands by prudence should be tied;
Venus in vain the wedded pair would crown,
If angry fortune on their union frown:
Soon will the flattering dream of bliss be o'er
And cloyed imagination cheat no more.
Then waking to the sense of lasting pain,
With mutual tears the nuptial couch they stain,
And that fond love, which should afford relief,
Does but increase the anguish of their grief,
While both could easier their own sorrows bear
Than the sad knowledge of each other's care.

EDWARD LITTLETON

On The Death Of Mrs Bowes

Hail, happy bride, for thou art truly blest!
Three months of rapture, crowned with endless rest.
Merit like yours was heaven's peculiar care,
You loved yet tasted happiness sincere.
To you the sweets of love were only shown,
The sure succeeding bitter dregs unknown;
You had not yet the fatal change deplored,
The tender lover for th' imperious lord:
Nor felt the pain that jealous fondness brings:
Nor felt that coldness from possession springs.
Above your sex, distinguished in your fate,
You trusted yet experienced no deceit;
Soft were your hours, and winged with pleasure flew;
No vain repentance gave a sigh to you:
And if superior bliss heaven can bestow,
With fellow angels you enjoy it now.

LADY MARY WORTLEY MONTAGU

Wedlock

(EXTRACT)

Eternal foe to soft desires,
Inflamer of forbidden fires,
Thou source of discord, pain and care,
Thou sure forerunner of despair,
Thou scorpion with a double face,
Thou lawful plague of human race,
Thou bane of freedom, ease and mirth,
Thou deep damnation upon earth,
Thou serpent which the angels fly,
Thou monster whom the beasts defy,
Whom wily Jesuits sneer at too;
And Satan (let him have his due)
Was never so confirmed a dunce

To risk damnation more than once.
That wretch, if such a wretch there be,
Who hopes for happiness from thee,
May search successfully as well
For truth in whores and ease in hell.

MEHETABEL WRIGHT

To My Friend Exillus

ON PERSUADING ME TO MARRY OLD DAMON

When friend's advice with lover's forces join
They'll conquer hearts more fortified than mine;
For mine lies as it wont, without defence,
No guard nor art but its own innocence;
Under which fort, it could fierce storms endure,
But from my wit I find no fort secure.
Ah, why wouldst thou assist my enemy,
Who was himself almost too strong for me?
Thou with idolatry mak'st me adore,
And homage do to the proud conqueror.
Now round his neck my willing arms I'd twine,
And swear upon his lips, My Dear, I'm thine.
But that his kindness then would grow, I fear,
Too weighty for my weak desert to bear.
I fear 't would even to extremes improve,
And jealousy, they say 's th'extreme of love;
That after all my kindness to him shown,
My little Neddy, he'll not think't his own:
Even thou my dear Exillus he'll suspect,
If I but look on thee, I him neglect:
Not only he-friends innocent as thou,
But he'll mistrust she-friends and heaven too.
Thus best things may be turned to greatest harm
As saying the Lord's Prayer backward proves a charm.
Or if not thus, I'm sure he will despise,
Or underrate the easy-gotten prize.

These and a thousand fears my soul possess,
But most of all my own unworthiness;
Like dying saints I wish for coming joys,
But humble fears that forward wish destroys.
What shall I do then? hazard the event?
You say, Old Damon's all that's excellent.
If I miss him, the next some squire may prove,
Whose dogs and horses shall have all his love;
Or some debauched pretender to lewd wit,
Or covetous, conceited, unbred citt.
Thus the brave horse, who late i' the coach did neigh
Is forced at last to tug a nasty dray.

                                        JANE BARKER

The Wife

She rose to his requirement, dropped
The playthings of her life
To take the honorable work
Of woman and of wife.

If aught she missed in her new day
Of amplitude, or awe,
Or first prospective, or the gold
In using wore away,

It lay unmentioned, as the sea
Develops pearl and weed,
But only to himself is known
The fathoms they abide.

                                  EMILY DICKINSON

In Praise Of The Single State

And I would praise them more, only I fear,
If I should do it, 't would make me appear
Unto the world much fonder than I be
Of that same state, for I love liberty.
Nor do I think there's a necessity
For all to enter beds, like Noah's beast
Into his ark. I would have some released
From the dear cares of that same lawful state;
But I'll not dictate, I'll leave all that to fate.

SARAH EGERTON

Marry Not In Haste

Take thus much of my counsel: marry not
In haste; for she that takes the best of husbands
Puts but on a golden fetter; for husbands
Are like to painted fruit, which promises much,
But still deceive us, when we come to touch.
If you match with a courtier, he'll have a
Dozen mistresses at least, and repent
His marriage within four and twenty hours
At most; swearing a wife, is fit for none
But an old justice, or a country gentleman:
If you marry a citizen, though you
Live never so honest, yet he shall be venturing
Abroad, when he might deal a great deal more
Safe at home. And this take of me, that 'mongst
The best, there is none good, all bad;
She's married best, that's wedded to her will.

ANONYMOUS

Thou Genius Of Connubial Love

Thou genius of connubial love, attend!
Let silent wonder all thy powers suspend,
Whilst to thy glory I devote my lays,
And pour forth all my grateful heart in praise.
    In lifeless strains let vulgar satire tell
That marriage oft is mixed with heaven and hell,
That conjugal delight is soured with spleen,
And peace and war compose the varied scene.
My muse a truth sublimer can assert,
And sing the triumphs of a mutual heart.

    Thrice happy they who through life's varied tide
With equal pace and gentle motion glide,
Whom, though the wave of fortune sinks or swells,
One reason governs and one wish impels,
Whose emulation is to love the best,
Who feels no bliss but in each other blessed,
Who knows no pleasure but the joys they give,
Nor cease to love but when they cease to live.
If fate these blessings in one lot combine,
Then let th' eternal page record them mine.

                              THOMAS BLACKLOCK

A Letter To Daphnis

This to the crown and blessing of my life,
The much loved husband of a happy wife;
To him whose constant passion found the art
To win a stubborn and ungrateful heart;
And to the world by tenderest proof discovers
They err, who say that husbands can't be lovers.
With such return of passion as is due,
Daphnis I love, Daphnis my thoughts pursue;
Daphnis my hopes and joys are bounded all in you.

Even I, for Daphnis' and my promise' sake,
What I in women censure, undertake.
But this from love, not vanity, proceeds;
You know who writes, and I who 'tis that reads.
Judge not my passion by my want of skill:
Many love well, though they express it ill;
And I your censure could with pleasure bear,
Would you but soon return, and speak it here.

ANN FINCH

A Marriage Ring

The ring so worn as you behold,
So thin, so pale, is yet of gold:
The passion such it was to prove;
Worn with life's cares, love yet was love.

GEORGE CRABBE

Verses Written On Her Death-Bed At Bath To Her Husband In London

Thou who dost all my worldly thoughts employ,
Thou pleasing source of all my earthly joy,
Thou tenderest husband and thou dearest friend,
To thee this first, this last adieu I send!
At length the conqueror death asserts his right,
And will for ever veil me from thy sight;
He woos me to him with a cheerful grace,
And not one terror clouds his meagre face;
He promises a lasting rest from pain,
And shows that all life's fleeting joys are vain;
Th' eternal scenes of heaven he sets in view;
And tells me that no other joys are true.

But love, fond love, would yet resist his power,
Would fain awhile defer the parting hour;
He brings thy mourning image to my eyes,
And would obstruct my journey to the skies.
But say, thou dearest, thou unwearied friend!
Say, shouldst thou grieve to see my sorrows end?
Thou know'st a painful pilgrimage I've passed;
And shouldst thou grieve that rest is come at last?
Rather rejoice to see me shake off life,
And die as I have lived, thy faithful wife.

MARY MONK

An Epitaph Upon Husband and Wife Who Died And Were Buried Together

To these whom death again did wed
This grave's the second marriage-bed.
For though the hand of fate could force
'Twixt soul and body a divorce,
It could not sever man and wife,
Because they both lived but one life.
Peace, good reader, do not weep;
Peace, the lovers are asleep.
They, sweet turtles, folded lie
In the last knot that love could tie.
Let them sleep, let them sleep on,
Till the stormy night be gone,
And the eternal morrow dawn;
Then the curtains will be drawn,
And they wake into a light
Whose day shall never die in night.

RICHARD CRASHAW

PARTING

Ae Fond Kiss

Ae fond kiss, and when we sever, –
Ae faerweel, and then – for ever!
Deep in heart-wrung tears I'll pledge thee!
Warring sighs and groans I'll wage thee!

Who shall say that fortune grieves him,
While the star of hope she leaves him?
Me, nae cheerfu' twinkle lights me, –
Dark despair around benights me.

I'll ne'er blame my partial fancy,
Naething could resist my Nancy;
But to see her was to love her –
Love but her, and love for ever.

Had we never lov'd sae kindly –
Had we never lov'd sae blindly –
Never met – or never parted,
We had ne'er been broken-hearted!

Fare-thee-weel, thou first and fairest!
Fare-thee-weel, thou best and dearest!
Thine be ilka joy and treasure,
Peace, enjoyment, love, and pleasure!

Ae fond kiss, and then we sever!
Ae fareweel, alas! for ever!
Deep in heart-wrung tears I'll pledge thee!
Warring sighs and groans I'll wage thee!

ROBERT BURNS

My Life Closed Twice

My life closed twice before its close;
    It yet remains to see
If immortality unveil
    A third event to me.

So huge, so hopeless to conceive,
    As these that twice befell.
Parting is all we know of heaven,
    And all we need of hell.

EMILY DICKINSON

Loth To Part

Heav'n knows how loth I am to part from thee:
So from the seal is softened wax disjoined:
So from the mother plant the under rind.

JOHN DRYDEN

When We Two Parted

When we two parted
    In silence and tears,
Half broken-hearted
    To sever for years,
Pale grew thy cheek and cold,
    Colder thy kiss;
Truly that hour foretold
    Sorrow to this.

The dew of the morning
    Sunk chill on my brow –
It felt like the warning
    Of what I feel now.
Thy vows are all broken,
    And light is thy fame;
I hear thy name spoken,
    And share in its shame.

They name thee before men,
    A knell to mine ear;
A shudder comes o'er me –
    Why wert thou so dear?
They know not I knew thee,
    Who knew thee too well:–
Long, long shall I rue thee,
    Too deeply to tell.

In secret we met –
    In silence I grieve,
That thy heart could forget,
    Thy spirit deceive.
If I should meet thee
    After long years,
How should I greet thee?–
    With silence and tears.

GEORGE GORDON, LORD BYRON

First Farewell To J.G.

Farewell my dearer half, you of my heart,
Heaven only knows how loth I am to part:
Whole months but hours seem, when you are here,
When absent, every minute is a year:
Might I but always see thy charming face,
I'd live on racks, and wish no easier place.
But we must part, your interest says we must;
Fate, me no longer with such treasure trust.

I would not tax you with inconstancy,
Yet Strephon, you are not so kind as I:
No interest, no nor fate itself has power
To tempt me from the idol I adore:
But since you needs will go, may Africk be
Kinder to you, than Europe is to me:
May all you meet and everything you view
Give you such transport as I met in you.
May no sad thoughts disturb your quiet mind,
Except you'll think of her you left behind.

'EPHELIA'

The Meeting

We started speaking,
Looked at each other, then turned away.
The tears kept rising to my eyes.
But I could not weep.
I wanted to take your hand
But my hand trembled.
You kept counting the days
Before we should meet again.
But both of us felt in our hearts
That we parted for ever and ever.
The ticking of the little clock filled the quiet room.
'Listen,' I said. 'It is so loud,
Like a horse galloping on a lonely road,
As loud as a horse galloping past in the night.'
You shut me up in your arms.
But the sound of the clock stifled our hearts' beating.
You said, 'I cannot go: all that is living of me
Is here for ever and ever.'
Then you went.
The world changed. The sound of the clock grew fainter,
Dwindled away, became a minute thing.
I whispered in the darkness, 'If it stops, I shall die.'

KATHERINE MANSFIELD

My Love And I Must Part

Weep eyes, break heart!
My love and I must part.
Cruel fates true love do soonest sever;
O, I shall see thee never, never, never!
O, happy is the maid whose life takes end
Ere it knows parent's frown or loss of friend!
Weep eyes, break heart!
My love and I must part.

THOMAS MIDDLETON

Penelope

Certain parting does not wait its hour
for separation; too soon the shadow lies
upon the heart and chokes the voice, its power
drives on the minutes, it implies
tomorrow while today's still here.

They sat by firelight and his shadow fell
for the last time, she thought, black patterning gold
sharp on the firelit wall. So, to compel
the evening to outlast the morning's cold
dawn by the quayside and the unshed tears,

she took a charred twig from the hearth and drew
the outline of his shadow on the wall.
'These were his features, this the hand I knew.'
She heard her voice saying the words through all
the future days of solitude and fear.

URSULA VAUGHAN WILLIAMS

On The Departure Platform

We kissed at the barrier; and passing through
She left me, and moment by moment got
Smaller and smaller, until to my view
    She was but a spot;

A wee white spot of muslin fluff
That down the diminishing platform bore
Through hustling crowds of gentle and rough
    To the carriage door.

Under the lamplight's fitful glowers,
Behind dark groups from far and near,
Whose interests were apart from ours,
    She would disappear.

Then show again, till I ceased to see
That flexible form, that nebulous white;
And she who was more than my life to me
    Had vanished quite . . .

We have penned new plans since that fair fond day,
And in season she will appear again —
Perhaps in the same soft white array —
    But never as then!

— 'And why, young man, must eternally fly
A joy you'll repeat, if you love her well?'
— O friend, nought happens twice thus: why,
    I cannot tell!

THOMAS HARDY

The Taxi

When I go away from you
The world beats dead
Like a slackened drum.
I call out for you against the jutted stars
And shout into the ridges of the wind.

Streets coming fast,
One after the other,
Wedge you away from me,
And the lamps of the city prick my eyes
So that I can no longer see your face.
Why should I leave you,
To wound myself upon the sharp edges of the night?

AMY LOWELL

Parting

IN PEACETIME

When we reached the gate I raised my eyes
And, kissing you good night, I laughed and said
I feared the stars might strike you from the skies,
Like crystal stones on your too happy head.

IN WARTIME

How long ago Hector took off his plume,
Not wanting that his little son should cry,
Then kissed his sad Andromache goodbye
And now we three in Euston waiting-room.

FRANCES CORNFORD

Worth Dying For

If we shall live, we live:
　　If we shall die; we die:
If we live we shall meet again:
　　But to-night, good-bye.
One word, let but one be heard –
　　What, not one word?

If we sleep we shall wake again
    And see to-morrow's light:
If we wake, we shall meet again:
    But to-night, good-night.
Good-night, my lost and found –
    Still not a sound?

    If we live, we must part;
If we die, we part in pain:
    If we die, we shall part
    Only to meet again.
By those tears on either cheek,
    To-morrow you will speak.

To meet, worth living for:
Worth dying for, to meet,
To meet, worth parting for:
Bitter forgot in sweet.
To meet, worth parting before,
Never to part more.

CHRISTINA ROSSETTI

Parting

(EXTRACT)

Darling, this is goodbye. The words are ordinary
But love is rare. So let it go tenderly
as the sound of violins into silence.

Parting is sad for us, because something is over,
But for the thing we have ended, it is a beginning –
Let love go like a young bird flying from the nest,

Like a new star, airborne into the evening,
Watched out of sight, or let it fall gently as a tear,
Let our love go out of the world, like the prayer for a soul's rest.

Let the roses go, that you fastened in my hair
One summer night in a garden, and the song

That we heard from another house, where a piano was playing:
The shadow at a street lamp cast through the net of a curtain,
The river at night, smooth silent Thames, flowing through London.

For two years Ullswater was silver with my love for you,
The golden birch-leaves were holy, the wild cherry was sweet
On the fell-sides, scenting the spring for you.
The bees, drunk with the lime-flowers, dropped like grapes
    on the road,
And the silence was yours, over all Westmorland at night.

I raised the mountains for you, and set the streams
Running down the hills for love. I saw the moss grow
And the ferns unroll their croziers for love of you,
The snowdrops, the primrose, the heron, the martin, the sheep on
    the fells.

. . . Yours, too, was the anterooom of the angels,
When I could hear a pin drop, or a drop of rain,
Or the creak of a beam, or a butterfly caught in the rafters.
I wrestled with angels for you, and in my body
Endured the entire blessing of love's pain.

All this is true. These things, my dear, are a life
Lived for love of you. The fire in the heart, the fire on the hearth,
And children's stories in the evening, even hope's death
Were precious for you. Precious all things in time
And outside time. The poem I know, and the wisdom
That is not mine, the poem that can never be written . . .

KATHLEEN RAINE

A Farewell

With all my will, but much against my heart,
We two now part,
My Very Dear,
Our solace is, the sad road lies so clear.
It needs no art,
With faint averted feet

And many a tear,
In our opposèd paths to persevere.
Go thou to east, I west.
We will not say
There's any hope, it is so far away.
But, O, my best,
When the one darling of our widowhead,
The nursling grief
Is dead,
And no dews blur our eyes
To see the peach-bloom come in evening skies,
Perchance we may,
Where now this night is day,
And even through faith of still averted feet,
Making full circle of our banishment,
Amazèd meet;
The bitter journey to the bourne so sweet
Seasoning the termless feast of our content
With tears of recognition never dry.

COVENTRY PATMORE

Love Me At Last

Love me at last, or if you will not,
Leave me;
Hard words could never, as these half words,
Grieve me:
Love me at last – or leave me.

Love me at last, or let the last word uttered
Be but your own;
Love me, or leave me – as a cloud, a vapor,
Or a bird flown.
Love me at last – I am but sliding water
Over a stone.

ALICE CORBIN

A Valediction

If we must part,
Then let it be like this;
Not heart on heart,
Nor with the useless anguish of a kiss;
But touch mine hand and say:
'Until to-morrow or some other day,
If we must part.'

Words are so weak
When love hath been so strong:
Let silence speak:
'Life is a little while, and love is long;
A time to sow and reap,
And after harvest a long time to sleep,
But words are weak.'

ERNEST DOWSON

The Request Of Alexis

Give, give me back that trifle you despise,
Give back my heart, with all its injuries:
Tho' by your cruelty it wounded be,
The thing is yet of wondrous use to me.
A gen'rous conqueror, when the battle's won,
Bestows a charity on the undone:
If from the well-aimed stroke no hope appear,
He kills the wretch, and shews compassion there:
But you, barbarian! keep alive in pain,
A lasting trophy of unjust disdain.

SARAH DIXON

The Gift

What can I give you, my lord, my lover,
You who have given the world to me,
Showed me the light and the joy that cover
The wild sweet earth and the restless sea?

All that I have are gifts of your giving —
If I gave them again, you would find them old,
And your soul would weary of always living
Before the mirror my life would hold.

What shall I give you, my lord, my lover?
The gift that breaks the heart in me:
I bid you awake at dawn and discover
I have gone my way and left you free.

SARA TEASDALE

Since There's No Help

Since there's no help, come let us kiss and part,
Nay, I have done; you get no more of me.
And I am glad, yea, glad with all my heart,
That thus so cleanly I myself can free.
Shake hands for ever; cancel all our vows.
And when we meet at any time again,
Be it not seen in either of our brows
That we one jot of former love retain.
Now, at the last gasp of love's latest breath,
When, his pulse failing, passion speechless lies,
When faith is kneeling by his bed of death,
And innocence is closing up his eyes, —
Now, if thou would'st, when all have given him over,
From death to life thou mightest him yet recover.

MICHAEL DRAYTON

To His Coy Love

I pray thee, leave, love me no more,
    Call home the heart you gave me!
I but in vain that saint adore
    That can but will not save me.
These poor half-kisses kill me quite —
    Was ever man thus servèd:
Amidst an ocean of delight
    For pleasure to be starvèd!

Show me no more those snowy breasts
    With azure riverets branchèd,
Where, whilst mine eye with plenty feasts,
    Yet is my thirst not stanchèd;
O Tantalus, thy pains ne'er tell!
    By me thou art prevented:
'Tis nothing to be plagued in hell,
    But thus in heaven tormented.

Clip me no more in those dear arms,
    Nor thy life's comfort call me,
O these are but too powerful charms,
    And do but more enthral me!
But see how patient I am grown
    In all this coil about thee:
Come, nice thing, let my heart alone,
    I cannot live without thee!

MICHAEL DRAYTON

THE END OF LOVE

Modern Love

(EXTRACT)

In our old shipwrecked days there was an hour,
When in the firelight steadily aglow,
Joined slackly, we beheld the red chasm grow
Among the clicking coals. Our library-bower
That eve was left to us: and hushed we sat
As lovers to whom time is whispering.
From sudden-opened doors we heard them sing.
The nodding elders mixed good wine with chat.
Well knew we that life's treasure lay
With us, and of it was our talk. 'Ah, yes!
Love dies!' I said: I never thought it less.
She yearned to me that sentence to unsay.
Then when the fire domed blackening, I found
Her cheek was salt against my kiss, and swift
Up the sharp scale of sobs her breast did lift: –
Now am I haunted by that taste! that sound!

GEORGE MEREDITH

Divided

They did not quarrel; but betwixt them came
Combining circumstances, urging on
Towards the final ending of their loves.
Could they have smote and stung with bitter words,
Then sued for pardon on a blotted page,
And met, and kissed, and dried their mutual tears,
This had not been. But every day the breach
Widened without their knowledge. Time went by,
And led their footsteps into devious paths,

Each one approving, nay, with waving hand
Praying God speed the other, since both roads
Seemed fair, and led away from sordid things,
And each one urged the other one to fame.
He was a very Caesar for ambition;
And she, a simple singer in the woods,
Athirst for Nature – ever needing her
To crown a holiday, and sanctify
As with a mother's blessing, idle hours.
A bramble-blossom trailing in the way
Seemed more to her than all his talk of courts
And kings and constitutions; but his aims
Rose far above the soaring of the lark,
That leaves the peeping daisy out of sight.
The state required him, and he could not stay
Loit'ring and ling'ring in the 'primrose path
Of dalliance'; and so it came to pass,
These two, that once were one, are two again.
And she is lone in spirit, having known
A sweeter thing than pipe of nightingale
Or scent of hawthorn, and yet loving these
And clinging to them still, though desolate,
And, like the lady of the 'Lord of Burleigh',
Lacking the 'Landscape-painter' in her life.
Thus, all her songs are sad – of withered leaves,
And blighted hopes, and echoes of the past,
And early death; and yet she cannot die,
But lives and sings, as he, too, lives and climbs,
Far from the sight of waving meadow-grass;
And so they walk divided.

      Were it well
So soon to sever such a tender tie,
With never a reproach and none to blame,
And not one tear? With friendly greetings now
At careless meetings, cold and unforeseen,
As though no better days had ever dawned;
And all – for what? . . .

Nay, be it for the best!
Who knows, if we love well till we regret
And sigh, in sadness, for a good thing gone?
Thus, all may work to wisdom.

Wherefore, wake
With wind-strewn cuckoo-bloom and daffodil,
Fond foolish love of spring-tide and hot youth,
And die when these have perished! . . .

VIOLET FANE

The Expiration

So, so, break off this last lamenting kiss,
    Which sucks two souls, and vapours both away,
Turn thou ghost that way, and let me turn this,
    And let our selves benight our happiest day,
We asked none leave to love; nor will we owe
    Any so cheap a death as saying, Go;

Go; and if that word have not quite killed thee,
    Ease me with death, by bidding me go too.
Oh, if it have, let my word work on me,
    And a just office on a murderer do.
Except it be too late, to kill me so,
    Being double dead, going, and bidding, go.

JOHN DONNE

Like The Touch Of Rain

Like the touch of rain she was
On a man's flesh and hair and eyes
When the joy of walking thus
Has taken him by surprise:

With the love of the storm he burns,
He sings, he laughs, well I know how,
But forgets when he returns
As I shall not forget her 'Go now'.

Those two words shut a door
Between me and the blessed rain
That was never shut before
And will not open again.

EDWARD THOMAS

The Surrender

My once dear love! hapless that I no more
Must call thee so; the rich affection's store
That fed our hopes lies now exhaust and spent,
Like sums of treasure unto bankrupts lent.

We, that did nothing study but the way
To love each other, with which thoughts the day
Rose with delight to us, and with them, set,
Must learn the hateful art how to forget.

We, that did nothing wish that heaven could give,
Beyond our selves, nor did desire to live
Beyond that wish, all these now cancel must,
As if not writ in faith, but words and dust.

Yet witness those clear vows which lovers make,
Witness the chaste desires that never break
Into unruly heats; witness that breast
Which in thy bosom anchored his whole rest,
'Tis not default in us, I dare acquite
Thy maiden faith, thy purpose fair and white,
As thy pure self. Cross planets did envy
Us to each other, and heaven did untie
Faster than vows could bind. O that the stars
When lovers meet, should stand opposed in wars!

Since then some higher destinies command
Let us not strive nor labour to withstand
What is past help. The longest date of grief
Can never yield a hope of our relief;
And though we waste ourselves in moist laments,
Tears may drown us, but not our discontents.

Fold back our arms, take home our fruitless loves,
That must new fortunes try, like turtle doves
Dislodged from their haunts. We must in tears
Unwind a love knit up in many years.
In this last kiss I here surrender thee
Back to thyself: so thou again art free.
Thou in another, sad as that, re-send
The truest heart that lover ere did lend . . .

HENRY KING

Farewell!

Farewell! thou art too dear for my possessing,
And like enough thou knowest thy estimate:
The charter of thy worth gives thee releasing;
My bonds in thee are all determinate.
For how do I hold thee but by thy granting?
And for that riches where is my deserving?
The cause of this fair gift in me is wanting,
And so my patent back again is swerving.
Thyself thou gavest, thy own worth then not knowing,
Or me, to whom thou gavest it, else mistaking;
So thy great gift, upon misprision growing,
Comes home again, on better judgement making.
　　Thus have I had thee, as a dream doth flatter,
　　In sleep a king, but waking no such matter.

WILLIAM SHAKESPEARE

Beyond

Love's aftermath! I think the time is now
That we must gather in, alone, apart
The saddest crop of all the crops that grow,
    Love's aftermath.
Ah, sweet, – sweet yesterday, the tears that start
Can not put back the dial; this is, I trow,
Our harvesting! Thy kisses chill my heart,
Our lips are cold; averted eyes avow
The twilight of poor love: we can but part,
Dumbly and sadly, reaping as we sow,
    Love's aftermath.

ERNEST DOWSON

The End Of The Episode

    Indulge no more may we
In this sweet-bitter pastime:
The love-light shines the last time
    Between you, Dear, and me.

    There shall remain no trace
Of what so closely tied us,
And blank as ere love eyed us
    Will be our meeting-place.

    The flowers and thymy air,
Will they now miss our coming?
The dumbles thin their humming
    To find we haunt not there?

    Though fervent was our vow,
Though ruddily ran our pleasure,
Bliss has fulfilled its measure,
    And sees its sentence now.

Ache deep; but make no moans:
Smile out; but stilly suffer:
The paths of love are rougher
    Than thoroughfares of stones.

THOMAS HARDY

The End Of It

She did not love to love, but hated him
For making her to love; and so her whim
From passion taught misprision to begin.
And all this sin
Was because love to cast out had no skill
Self, which was regent still.
Her own self-will made void her own self's will.

FRANCIS THOMPSON

Farewell

It is buried and done with
    The love that we knew:
Those cobwebs we spun with
    Are beaded with dew.

I loved thee; I leave thee:
    To love thee was pain:
I dare not believe thee
    To love thee again.

Like spectres unshriven
    Are the years that I lost;
To thee they were given
    Without count of cost.

I cannot revive them
    By penance or prayer;
Hell's tempest must drive them
    Thro' turbulent air.

Farewell, and forget me:
    For I too am free
From the shame that beset me,
    The sorrow of thee.

JOHN ADDINGTON SYMONDS

A Separation Deed

Whereas we twain, who still are bound for life,
Who took each other for better and for worse,
Are now plunged deep in hate and bitter strife,
And all our former love is grown a curse;
So that 'twere better, doubtless, we should be
In loneliness, so that we were apart,
Nor in each other's changed eyes looking, see
The cold reflection of an alien heart:
To this insensate parchment we reveal
Our joint despair, and seal it with our seal.

Forgetting the dear days not long ago,
When we walked slow by starlight through the corn:
Forgetting, since our hard fate wills it so,
All but our parted lives and souls forlorn;
Forgetting the sweet fetters strong to bind
Which childish fingers forge, and baby smiles,
Our common pride to watch the growing mind,
Our common joy in childhood's simple wiles,
The common tears we shed, the kiss we gave,
Standing beside the open little grave.

Forgetting these and more, if to forget
Be possible, as we would fain indeed.
And if the past be not too deeply set
In our two hearts, with roots that, touched, will bleed

Yet, could we cheat by any pretext fair
The world, if not ourselves — 'twere so far well —
We would not put our bonds from us, and bare
To careless eyes the secrets of our hell;
So this indenture witnesseth that we,
As follows here, do solemnly agree.

We will take each our own, and will abide
Separate from bed and board for all our life;
Whatever chance of weal or woe betide,
Naught shall re-knit the husband and the wife.
Though one grow gradually poor and weak,
The other, lapt in luxury, will not heed;
Though one, in mortal pain, the other seek,
The other may not answer to the need;
We, who thro' long years did together rest
In wedlock, heart to heart, and breast to breast.

One shall the daughter take, and one the boy, —
Poor boy, who shall not hear his mother's name,
Nor feel her kiss; poor girl, for whom the joy
Of her sire's smile is changed for sullen shame:
Brother and sister, who, if they should meet,
With faces strange, amid the careless crowd,
Will feel their hearts beat with no quicker beat,
Nor inward voice of kinship calling loud:
Two widowed lives, whose fullness may not come;
Two orphan lives, knowing but half of home.

We have not told the tale, nor will, indeed,
Of dissonance, whether cruel wrong or crime,
Or sum of petty injuries which breed
The hate of hell when multiplied by time,
Dishonour, falsehood, jealous fancies, blows,
Which in one moment wedded souls can sunder;
But, since our yoke intolerable grows,
Therefore we set our seals and souls as under:
Witness the powers of wrong and hate and death.
And this indenture also witnesseth.

SIR LEWIS MORRIS

Dead Love

Oh never weep for love that's dead
Since love is seldom true
But changes his fashion from blue to red,
From brightest red to blue,
And love was born to an early death
And is so seldom true.

Then harbour no smile on your bonny face
To win the deepest sigh.
The fairest words on truest lips
Pass on and surely die,
And you will stand alone, my dear,
When wintry winds draw nigh.

Sweet, never weep for what cannot be,
For this God has not given.
If the merest dream of love were true
Then, sweet, we should be in heaven,
And this is only earth, my dear,
Where true love is not given.

ELIZABETH SIDDAL

O Joy Of Love's Renewing

O joy of love's renewing,
　　Could love be born again;
Relenting for thy rueing,
　　And pitying my pain:
O joy of love's awaking,
　　Could love arise from sleep,
Forgiving our forsaking
　　The fields we would not reap!

Fleet, fleet we fly, pursuing
    The love that fled amain,
But will he list our wooing,
    Or call we but in vain?
Ah! vain is all our wooing,
    And all our prayers are vain,
Love listeth not our suing,
    Love will not wake again.

ANDREW LANG

Parting Well

Phillis, let's shun the common fate,
And let our love ne'er turn to hate;
I'll dote no longer than I can,
Without being called a faithless man.
When we begin to want discourse,
And kindness seems to taste of force,
As freely as we met we'll part,
Each one possessed of their own heart.
Thus, whilst rash fools themselves undo,
We'll game and give off savers too;
So equally the match we'll make
Both shall be glad to draw the stake.
A smile of thine shall make my bliss,
I will enjoy thee in a kiss:
If from this height our kindness fall,
We'll bravely scorn to love at all:
If thy affection first decay,
I will the blame on nature lay.
Alas, what cordial can remove
The hasty fate of dying love?
Thus we will all the world excel
In loving and in parting well.

SIR CHARLES SEDLEY

Ephemera

'Your eyes that once were never weary of mine
Are bowed in sorrow under pendulous lids,
Because our love is waning.'
                     And then she:
'Although our love is waning, let us stand
By the lone border of the lake once more,
Together in that hour of gentleness
When the poor tired child, Passion, falls asleep:
How far away the stars seem, and how far
Is our first kiss, and ah, how old my heart!'

Pensive they paced along the faded leaves,
While slowly he whose hand held hers replied:
'Passion has often worn our wandering hearts.'

The woods were round them, and the yellow leaves
Fell like faint meteors in the gloom, and once
A rabbit old and lame limped down the path;
On the lone border of the lake once more:
Turning, he saw that she had thrust dead leaves
Gathered in silence, dewy as her eyes,
In bosom and hair.
                'Ah, do not mourn,' he said,
'That we are tired, for other loves await us;
Hate on and love through unrepining hours.
Before us lies eternity; our souls
Are love, and a continual farewell.'

W.B. YEATS

Maturity

All love at first, like generous wine,
Ferments and frets until 'tis fine;
But when 'tis settled on the lee
And from the impurer matter free,
Becomes the richer still, the older,
And proves the pleasanter, the colder.

SAMUEL BUTLER

The Fire Of Love

The fire of love in youthful blood
Like what is kindled in brushwood,
    But for a moment burns;
Yet, in that moment, makes a mighty noise:
It crackles, and to vapour turns,
    And soon itself destroys,

But, when crept into aged veins,
It slowly burns, and long remains,
    And, with a silent heat,
Like fire in logs, it glows and warms 'em long!
And tho' the flame be not so great,
    Yet is the heat as strong.

CHARLES SACKVILLE, EARL OF DORSET

He That Loves A Rosy Cheek

He that loves a rosy cheek,
   Or a coral lip admires,
Or from star-like eyes doth seek
   Fuel to maintain his fires;
As old Time makes these decay,
So his flames must waste away.

But a smooth and steadfast mind,
   Gentle thoughts and calm desires,
Hearts with equal love combined,
   Kindle never-dying fires;
Where these are not, I despise
Lovely cheeks, or lips, or eyes.

THOMAS CAREW

The Marriage Of True Minds

Let me not to the marriage of true minds
Admit impediments: love is not love
Which alters when it alteration finds,
Or bends with the remover to remove.
O, no! it is an ever-fixèd mark,
That looks on tempests and is never shaken;
It is the star to every wandering bark,
Whose worth's unknown, although his height be taken.
Love's not Time's fool, though rosy lips and cheeks
Within his bending sickle's compass come;
Love alters not with his brief hours and weeks,
But bears it out even to the edge of doom.
   If this be error and upon me proved,
   I never writ, nor no man ever loved.

WILLIAM SHAKESPEARE

The Reconcilement

Come, let us now resolve at last
    To live and love in quiet;
We'll tie the knot so very fast
    That Time shall ne'er untie it.

The truest joys they seldom prove
    Who free from quarrels live:
'Tis the most tender part of love
    Each other to forgive.

When least I seemed concerned, I took
    No pleasure, nor no rest;
And when I feigned an angry look,
    Alas! I loved you best.

Own but the same to me – you'll find
    How blest will be our fate.
O to be happy – to be kind –
    Sure never is too late!

JOHN SHEFFIELD, DUKE OF BUCKINGHAM

A Song Of A Young Lady To Her Ancient Lover

Ancient person, for whom I
All the flattering youth defy,
Long it be ere thou grow old,
Aching, shaking, crazy, cold,
But still continue as thou art,
Ancient person of my heart.

On thy withered lips and dry,
Which like barren furrows lie,
Brooding kisses I will pour
Shall thy youthful heat restore.
Such kind showers in Autumn fall,
And a second Spring recall,
Nor from thee will ever part,
Ancient person of my heart.

Thy nobler part, which but to name,
In our sex would be counted shame,
By age's frozen grasp possessed,
From his ice shall be released,
And, soothed by my reviving hand,
In former warmth and vigour stand.
All a lover's wish can reach,
For thy joy my love shall teach,
And for thy pleasure shall improve
All that art can add to love.
Yet still I love thee without art,
Ancient person of my heart.

JOHN WILMOT, EARL OF ROCHESTER

To His Mistress Confined

Think not, my Phoebe, 'cause a cloud
Doth now thy heavenly beauty shroud,
     My wandering eye
Can stoop to common beauties of the sky.
   Be thou but kind, and this eclipse
   Shall neither hinder eyes nor lips;
     For we will meet
Within our hearts, and kiss, where none shall see't.

Nor canst thou in thy prison be
Without some loving signs of me:
  When thou dost spy
A sunbeam peep into thy room, 'tis I
 For I am hid within that flame,
  And thus unto thy chamber came
   To let thee see
In what a martyrdom I burn for thee.

There's no sad picture that doth dwell
Upon the arras wall, but well
  Resembles me.
No matter though our years do not agree,
 Love can make old, as well as time,
  And he that doth but twenty climb,
   If he will prove
As true as I, shows fourscore years in love.

ABRAHAM COWLEY

To My Young Lover

Incautious youth, why dost thou so misplace
Thy fine encomiums on an o'er-blown face;
Which after all the varnish of thy quill,
Its pristine wrinkles show apparent still:
Nor is it in the power of youth to move
An age-chilled heart to any strokes of love.
Then choose some budding beauty, which in time
May crown thy wishes in thy blooming prime:
For nought can make a more preposterous show,
Than April's flowers stuck on St. Michael's bow.
To consecrate thy first-born sighs to me,
A superannuated deity;
Makes that idolatry and deadly sin,
Which otherwise had only venial been.

JANE BARKER

The Last Fruit Of Our Affection

From DEVIL'S LAW CASE

. . . O, I shall run mad!
For as we love our youngest children best,
So the last fruit of our affection,
Wherever we bestow it, is most strong,
Most violent, most unresistable,
Since 'tis indeed our latest harvest-home,
Last merriment 'fore winter . . .'

JOHN WEBSTER

I Look Into My Glass

I look into my glass,
And view my wasting skin,
And say, 'Would God it came to pass
My heart had shrunk as thin!'

For then, I, undistressed
By hearts grown cold to me,
Could lonely wait my endless rest
With equanimity.

But time, to make me grieve,
Part steals, lets part abide;
And shakes this fragile frame at eve
With throbbings of noontide.

THOMAS HARDY

October Tune

O love, turn from the unchanging sea, and gaze
Down these grey slopes upon the year grown old,
A-dying mid the autumn-scented haze
That hangeth o'er the hollow in the wold,
Where the wind-bitten ancient elms infold
Grey church, long barn, orchard, and red-roofed stead,
Wrought in dead days for men a long while dead.

Come down, O love; may not our hands still meet,
Since still we live today, forgetting June,
Forgetting May, deeming October sweet —
– Oh hearken, hearken! through the afternoon,
The grey tower sings a strange old tinkling tune!
Sweet, sweet, and sad, the toiling year's last breath,
Too satiate of life to strive with death.

And we too – will it not be soft and kind,
That rest from life, from patience and from pain,
That rest from bliss we know not when we find,
That rest from love which ne'er the end can gain? –
– Hark, how the tune swells, that erewhile did wane!
Look up, love! – ah, cling close and never move!
How can I have enough of life and love?

WILLIAM MORRIS

In Age I Bud Again

From THE FLOWER

Who would have thought my shrivelled heart
Could have recovered greenness? It was gone
    Quite underground, as flowers depart
To feed their mother-root when they have blown,
      Where they together
      All the hard weather,
Dead to the world, keep house unknown.

These are the wonders, Lord of Power,
Killing and quickening, bringing down to hell
    And up to heaven in an hour;
Making a chiming of a passing-bell.
      We say amiss,
      This or that is:
Thy word is all, if we could spell . . .

And now in age I bud again,
After so many deaths I live and write;
    I once more smell the dew and rain,
And relish versing: O my only light,
      It cannot be
      That I am he
On whom thy tempests fell all night.

GEORGE HERBERT

Youth And Beauty

Thou art so fair, and young withal,
    Thou kindl'st young desires in me,
Restoring life to leaves that fall,
    And sight to eyes that hardly see
    Half those fresh beauties bloom in thee.

Those, under sev'ral herbs and flow'rs
    Disguised, were all Medea gave,
When she recalled time's flying hours,
    And aged Aeson from his grave,
    For beauty can both kill and save.

Youth it enflames, but age it cheers,
    I would go back, but not return
To twenty but to twice those years;
    Not blaze, but ever constant burn,
    For fear my cradle prove my urn.

AURELIAN TOWNSEND

Friendship After Love

After the fierce midsummer all ablaze
    Has burned itself to ashes, and expires
    In the intensity of its own fires,
There come the mellow, mild, St Martin days
Crowned with the calm of peace, but sad with haze.
    So after love has led us, till he tires
    Of his own throes, and torments, and desires,
Comes large-eyed friendship: with a restful gaze,
He beckons us to follow, and across
    Cool verdant vales we wander free from care.
    Is it a touch of frost lies in the air?
Why are we haunted with a sense of loss?
We do not wish the pain back, or the heat;
And yet, and yet, these days are incomplete.

ELLA WHEELER WILCOX

Twilight

That time of year thou mayst in me behold
When yellow leaves, or none, or few, do hang
Upon these boughs which shake against the cold,
Bare ruined choirs, where late the sweet birds sang.
In me thou sees the twilight of such day
As after sunset fadeth in the west,
Which by and by black night doth take away,
Death's second self, that seals up all in rest.
In me thou seest the glowing of such fire
That on the ashes of his youth doth lie,
As the death-bed whereon it must expire,
Consumed with that which it was nourished by.
This thou perceivest, which makes thy love more strong
To love that well which thou must leave ere long.

WILLIAM SHAKESPEARE

A Passion Still More Deeply Charming

From AGAMEMNON

I know a passion still more deeply charming
Than fevered youth e'er felt; and that is love,
By long experience mellowed into friendship.
How far beyond that forward child of fancy?
With beauty pleased a-while, anon disgusted,
Seeking some other toy; how far more noble
Is that bright offspring of unchanging reason,
That fonder grows with age, and charms for ever.

JAMES THOMSON

LOVE BEREFT

The Moon Was A-Waning

The moon was a-waning,
  The tempest was over;
Fair was the maiden,
  And fond was the lover;
But the snow was so deep,
  That his heart it grew weary,
And he sunk down to sleep,
  In the moorland so dreary.

Soft was the bed
  She had made for her lover,
White were the sheets
  And embroidered the cover;
But his sheets are more white,
  And his canopy grander,
And sounder he sleeps
  Where the hill foxes wander.

Alas, pretty maiden,
  What sorrows attend you!
I see you sit shivering,
  With lights at your window;
But long may you wait
  Ere your arms shall enclose him,
For still, still he lies
  With a wreath on his bosom!

How painful the task
   The sad tidings to tell you! –
An orphan you were
   Ere this misery befell you;
And far in yon wild,
   Where the dead-tapers hover,
So cold, cold and wan
   Lies the corpse of your lover!

JAMES HOGG

The Widow Of Glencoe

(EXTRACT)

Do not lift him from the bracken,
   Leave him lying where he fell –
Better bier ye cannot fashion:
   None beseems him half so well
As the bare and broken heather,
   And the hard and trampled sod,
Whence his angry soul ascended
   To the judgement-seat of God!

. . . Tremblingly we scooped the covering
   From each kindred victim's head,
And the living lips were burning
   On the cold ones of the dead.
And I left them with their dearest –
   Dearest charge had every one –
Left the maiden with her lover,
   Left the mother with her son.
I alone of all was mateless –
   Far more wretched I than they,
For the snow would not discover
   Where my lord and husband lay.
But I wandered up the valley,
   Till I found him lying low,
With the gash upon his bosom
And the frown upon his brow –

Till I found him lying murdered,
    Where he wooed me long ago!
Women's weakness shall not shame me
    Why should I have tears to shed?
Could I rain them down like water,
    O my hero! on thy head –
Could the cry of lamentation
    Wake thee from thy silent sleep,
Could it set thy heart a throbbing,
    It were mine to wail and weep!
But I will not waste my sorrow,
    Lest the Campbell women say
That the daughters of Clanranald
    Are as weak and frail as they.

. . . Other eyes than mine shall glisten,
    Other hearts be rent in twain,
Ere the heathbells on thy hillock
    Wither in the autumn rain.
Then I'll seek thee where thou sleepest,
    And I'll veil my weary head,
Praying for a place beside thee,
    Dearer than my bridal-bed:
And I'll give thee tears, my husband!
    If the tears remain to me,
When the widows of the foemen
    Cry the coronach for thee!

WILLIAM AYTOUN

The Lover Laments
The Death Of His Love

The pillar perished is whereto I leant,
The strongest stay of mine unquiet mind:
The like of it no man again can find,
From east to west still seeking though he went
To mine unhap for hap away hath rent

Of all my joy the very bark and rind,
And I, alas, by chance am thus assigned
Daily to mourn till death do it relent.
But since that thus it is by destiny,
What can I more but have a woeful heart,
My pen in plaint, my voice in careful cry,
My mind in woe, my body full of smart.
And I myself, myself always to hate,
Till dreadful death do ease my doleful state?

                                        SIR THOMAS WYATT

Without Him

'*Senza te son nulla*' – PETRARCH

I touched the heart that loved me, as a player
    Touches a lyre; content with my poor skill
    No touch save mine knew my belov'd (and still
I thought at times: Is there no sweet lost air
Old loves could wake in him, I cannot share?);
    Oh, he alone, alone could so fulfil
    My thoughts in sound to the measure of my will.
He is dead, and silence takes me unawares.

The songs I knew not he resumes, set free
From my constraining love, alas for me!
    His part in our tune goes with him; my part
I locked in me for ever; I stand as mute
    As one with full strung music in his heart
Whose fingers stray upon a shattered lute.

                                        ALICE MEYNELL

Fragment

Master in loving! till we met
I lacked the pattern thy sweet love hath set:
I hear Death's footstep – must we then forget? –
    Stay, stay – not yet!

GEORGE ELIOT

Durisdeer

We'll meet nae mair at sunset, when the weary day is dune,
Nor wander hame thegither, by the lee licht o' the mune!
I'll hear your step nae longer amang the dewy corn,
For we'll meet nae mair, my bonniest, either at eve or morn.

The yellow broom is waving, abune the sunny brae,
And the rowan berries dancing, where the sparkling waters play.
Tho' a' is bright and bonnie, it's an eerie place to me,
For we'll meet nae mair, my dearest, either by burn or tree.

Far up into the wild hills, there's a kirkyard auld and still,
Where the frosts lie ilka morning, and the mists hang low and chill,
And there ye sleep in silence, while I wander here my lane,
Till we meet ance mair in heaven, never to part again.

LADY JOHN SCOTT

Bereavement

What doth it serve to see sun's burning face?
And skies enamelled with both Indies' gold?
Or moon at night in jettie chariot rolled?
And all the glory of that starry place?
What doth it serve earth's beauty to behold?
The mountain's pride, the meadow's flowery grace;

The stately comeliness of forests old,
The sport of clouds which would themselves embrace?
What doth it serve to heare the sylvan songs
The wanton mearle*, the nightingale's sad strains,
Which in dark shades seem to deplore my wrongs?
For what doth serve all that this world contains,
    Since she for whom those once to me were dear
    No part of them can have now with me here.

WILLIAM DRUMMOND

*blackbird

On Such A Day

    Some hang above the tombs,
    Some weep in empty rooms,
    I, when the iris blooms,
      Remember.

    I, when the cyclamen
    Opens her buds again,
    Rejoice a moment – then
      Remember.

MARY COLERIDGE

Highland Mary

Ye banks, and braes, and streams around,
    The castle o' Montgomery,
Green be your woods, and fair your flowers,
    Your waters never drumlie!*
There simmer first unfald her robes,
    And there the langest tarry:
For there I took the last fareweel
    O' my sweet Highland Mary.

How sweetly bloomed the gay green birk,
   How rich the hawthorn's blossom!
As underneath their fragrant shade,
   I clasped her to my bosom!
The golden hours, on angel wings,
   Flew o'er me and my dearie;
For dear to me as light and life,
   Was my sweet Highland Mary.

Wi' mony a vow, and locked embrace,
   Our parting was fu' tender;
And, pledging aft to meet again,
   We tore oursels asunder;
But Oh! fell death's untimely frost,
   That nipt my flower sae early!
Now green's the sod, and cauld's the clay,
   That wraps my Highland Mary!

O pale, pale now, those rosy lips
   I aft hae kiss'd sae fondly!
And clos'd for ay the sparkling glance,
   That dwelt on me sae kindly;
And mouldering now in silent dust
   That heart that lo'ed me dearly!
But still within my bosom's core,
   Shall live my Highland Mary.

                 ROBERT BURNS

*murky

Auld Robin Forbes

(EXTRACT)

When the clock had struck eight I expected him heame,
And wheyles went to meet him as far as Dumleane;
Of aw hours it telt eight was dearest to me,
But now when it streykes there's a tear i' my ee.

O Willy! dear Willy! it never can be
That age, time, or death, can divide thee and me!
For that spot on earth that's aye dearest to me,
Is the turf that has covered my Willy frae me!

SUSANNA BLAMIRE

To The Memory

OF THAT WORTHY MAN LIEUT. NATHANAEL BURT OF SPRINGFIELD
. . . [WHO DIED] IN THE BATTLE OF LAKE GEORGE IN THE RETREAT,
SEPTEMBER 8TH, 1783

Oh! – he – is – gone.

MARTHA BREWSTER

Cold In The Earth

Cold in the earth – and the deep snow piled above thee!
Far, far removed, cold in the dreary grave!
Have I forgot, my only love, to love thee,
Severed at last by time's all-severing wave?

Now, when alone, do my thoughts no longer hover
Over the mountains, on that northern shore,
Resting their wings where heath and fern-leaves cover
Thy noble heart for ever, ever more?

Cold in the earth, and fifteen wild Decembers
From those brown hills have melted into spring:
Faithful indeed is the spirit that remembers
After such years of change and suffering!

Sweet love of youth, forgive if I forget thee
While the world's tide is bearing me along:
Sterner desires and darker hopes beset me,
Hopes which obscure, but cannot do thee wrong!

No later light has lightened up my heaven,
No second morn has ever shone for me;
All my life's bliss from thy dear life was given,
All my life's bliss is in the grave with thee.

But when the days of golden dreams had perished,
And even despair was powerless to destroy,
Then did I learn how existence could be cherished,
Strengthened and fed without the aid of joy.

Then did I check the tears of useless passion –
Weaned my young soul from yearning after thine;
Sternly denied its burning wish to hasten
Down to that tomb already more than mine.

And, even yet, I dare not let it languish,
Dare not indulge in memory's rapturous pain;
Once drinking deep of that divinest anguish,
How could I seek the empty world again?

EMILY BRONTË

Douglas, Douglas, Tender And True

Could you come back to me, Douglas, Douglas,
In the old likeness that I knew,
I would be so faithful, so loving, Douglas,
Douglas, Douglas, tender and true.

Never a scornful word should grieve ye,
I'd smile on ye sweet as the angels do; –
Sweet as your smile on me shone ever,
Douglas, Douglas, tender and true.

Oh, to call back the days that are not!
My eyes were blinded, your words were few;
Do you know the truth now up in heaven,
Douglas, Douglas, tender and true?

I never was worthy of you, Douglas;
Not half worthy the like of you:
Now all men beside seem to me like shadows –
I love you, Douglas, tender and true.

Stretch out your hand to me, Douglas, Douglas,
Drop forgiveness from heaven like dew;
As I lay my heart on your dead heart, Douglas,
Douglas, Douglas, tender and true.

DINAH MARIA CRAIK

Parted

Farewell to one now silenced quite,
Sent out of hearing, out of sight,
My friend of friends, whom I shall miss.
He is not banished, though, for this,
Nor he, nor sadness, nor delight.

Though I shall talk with him no more,
A low voice sounds upon the shore.
He must not watch my resting-place,
But who shall drive a mournful face
From the sad winds about my door?

I shall not hear his voice complain,
But who shall stop the patient rain?
His tears must not disturb my heart,
But who shall change the years, and part
The world from every thought of pain?

Although my life is left so dim,
The morning crowns the mountain-rim;
Joy is not gone from summer-skies,
Nor innocence from children's eyes,
And all these things are part of him.

He is not banished, for the showers
Yet wake this green warm earth of ours.
How can the summer be sweet?
I shall not have him at my feet,
And yet my feet are on the flowers.

ALICE MEYNELL

The Azalea

There, where the sun shines first
Against our room,
She train'd the gold azalea, whose perfume
She, spring-like, from her breathing grace dispersed.
Last night the delicate crests of saffron bloom,
For this their dainty likeness watch'd and nurst,
Were just at point to burst.
At dawn I dream'd, O God, that she was dead,
And groan'd aloud upon my wretched bed,
And waked, ah, God, and did not waken her,
But lay, with eyes still closed,
Perfectly bless'd in the delicious sphere
By which I knew so well that she was near,
My heart to speechless thankfulness composed.
Till 'gan to stir
A dizzy somewhat in my troubled head –
It was the azalea's breath, and she was dead!
The warm night had the lingering buds disclosed,
And I had fall'n asleep with to my breast
A chance-found letter pressed
In which she said,
'So, till to-morrow eve, my own, adieu!
Parting's well-paid with soon again to meet,
Soon in your arms to feel so small and sweet,
Sweet to myself that am so sweet to you!'

COVENTRY PATMORE

The Voice

Woman much missed, how you call to me, call to me,
Saying that now you are not as you were
When you had changed from the one who was all to me,
But as at first, when our day was fair.

Can it be you that I hear? Let me view you, then,
Standing as when I drew near to the town
Where you would wait for me: yes, as I knew you then,
Even to the original air-blue gown!

Or is it only the breeze, in its listlessness
Travelling across the wet mead to me here,
You being ever dissolved to wan wistlessness,
Heard no more again far or near?

    Thus I; faltering forward,
    Leaves around me falling,
Wind oozing thin through the thorn from norward,
    And the woman calling.

THOMAS HARDY

Her Name Is At My Tongue

Her name is at my tongue whene'er I speak,
    Her shape's before my eyes where'er I stir,
Both day and night, as if her ghost did walk,
    And not she me, but I had murdered her.

PHILIP AYRES

Go By, Go By

Come not, when I am dead,
    To drop thy foolish tears upon my grave,
To trample round my fallen head,
    And vex the unhappy dust thou wouldst not save.
There let the wind sleep and the plover cry;
    But thou, go by.

Child, if it were thine error or thy crime
    I care no longer, being all unblest:
Wed whom thou wilt, but I am sick of time,
    And I desire to rest.
Pass on, weak heart, and leave me where I lie;
    Go by, go by.

ALFRED, LORD TENNYSON

Remember

Remember me when I am gone away,
Gone far away into the silent land;
When you can no more hold me by the hand,
Nor I half turn to go yet turning stay.
Remember me when no more day by day
You tell me of our future that you planned:
Only remember me; you understand
It will be late to counsel then or pray.
Yet if you should forget me for a while
And afterwards remember, do not grieve:
For if the darkness and corruption leave
A vestige of the thoughts that once I had,
Better by far you should forget and smile
Than that you should remember and be sad.

CHRISTINA ROSSETTI

No Longer Mourn For Me

No longer mourn for me when I am dead
Than you shall hear the surly sullen bell
Give warning to the world that I am fled
From this vile world, with vilest worm to dwell:
Nay, if you read this line, remember not
The hand that writ it; for I love you so,
That I in your sweet thoughts would be forgot,
If thinking on me then should make you woe.
O, if, I say, you look upon this verse
When I perhaps compounded am with clay,
Do not so much as my poor name rehearse,
But let your love even with my life decay,
    Lest the wise world should look into your moan
    And mock you with me after I am gone.

WILLIAM SHAKESPEARE

Midnight Lamentation

When you and I go down
Breathless and cold,
Our faces both worn back
To earthly mould,
How lonely we shall be!
What shall we do,
You without me,
I without you?

I cannot bear the thought
You, first, may die,
Nor of how you will weep,
Should I.
We are too much alone;
What can we do
To make our bodies one:
You, me; I, you?

We are most nearly born
Of one same kind;
We have the same delight,
The same true mind.
Must we then part, we part;
Is there no way
To keep a beating heart,
And light of day?

I could now rise and run
Through street on street
To where you are breathing – you,
That we might meet,
And that your living voice
Might sound above
Fear, and we two rejoice
Within our love.

How frail the body is,
And we are made
As only in decay
To lean and fade.
I think too much of death;
There is a gloom
When I can't hear your breath
Calm in some room.

Oh, but how suddenly
Either may droop;
Countenance be so white,
Body stoop.
Then there may be a place
Where fading flowers
Drop on a lifeless face
Through weeping hours.

Is, then, nothing safe?
Can we not find
Some everlasting life
In our one mind?
I feel it like disgrace
Only to understand
Your spirit through your word,
Or by your hand.

I cannot find a way
Through love and through;
I cannot reach beyond
Body, to you.
When you or I must go
Down evermore,
There'll be no more to say
— But a locked door.

HAROLD MONRO

Smile Through Thy Tears

Smile through thy tears, like the blush moss-rose,
    When the warm rains fall around it;
Thy fond heart now may seek repose
    From the rankling griefs that wound it.
For a parent's loss the eye may fill
    And weep till the heart runs over;
But the pang is longer and deeper still
    That wails o'er the grave of a lover.

Smile through thy tears, like the pale primrose
   When the zephyrs play around it;
In me let thy trembling heart repose;
   I will ward the sorrows that wound it.
Ah! vain were the wish, such love to crave
   As warmed thy maiden bosom
Ere Henry slept, where the alders wave
   O'er the night-shade's drooping blossom.

THOMAS LYLE

Many In Aftertimes

Vien dietro a me e lascia dir le genti. – DANTE
Contando i casi della vita nostra. – PETRARCA

Many in aftertimes will say of you
   'He loved her' – while of me what will you say?
   Not that I loved you more than just in play,
For fashion's sake as idle women do.
Even let them prate; who know not what we knew
   Of love and parting in exceeding pain.
   Of parting hopeless here to meet again,
Hopeless on earth, and heaven is out of view.
But by my heart of love laid bare to you.
   My love that you can make not void nor vain,
Love that foregoes you but to claim anew
   Beyond this passage of the gate of death,
I charge you at the Judgement make it plain
   My love of you was life and not a breath.

CHRISTINA ROSSETTI

The Legacy

My dearest love! when thou and I must part
And th' icy hand of death shall seize that heart
Which is all thine; within some spacious will
I'll leave no blanks for legacies to fill:
'Tis my ambition to die one of those
Who but himself hath nothing to dispose.
And since that is already thine, what need
I to re-give it by some newer deed?
Yet take it once again, free circumstance
Does oft the value of mean things advance:
Who thus repeats what he bequeathed before,
Proclaims his bounty richer than his store.
But let me not upon my love bestow
What is not worth the giving. I do owe
Somewhat to dust: my body's pampered care
Hungry corruption and the worm will share.
That mould'ring relic which in earth must lie
Would prove a gift of horror to thine eye
With this cast rag of my mortality
Let all my faults and errors buried be.
And as thy fear-cloth rots, so may kind fate
Those worst acts of my life incinerate.
He shall in story fill a glorious room
Whose ashes and whose sins sleep in one tomb.
If now to my cold hearse thou deign to bring
Some melting sighs as thy last offering,
My peaceful exequies are crowned, nor shall
I ask more honour at my funeral.
Thou wilt more richly balm me with thy tears
Then all the nard fragrant Arabia bears.
And as the Paphian Queen by her griefs shower
Brought up her dead love's spirit in a flower:
So by those precious drops rained from thine eyes,
Out of my dust, O may some virtue rise!
And like thy better genius thee attend,
Till thou in my dark period shalt end.

Lastly, my constant truth let me commend
To him thou choosest next to be thy friend.
For (witness all things good) I would not have
Thy youth and beauty married to my grave,
'Twould show thou didst repent the style of wife
Should'st thou relapse into a single life.
They with preposterous grief the world delude
Who mourn for their lost mates in solitude;
Since widowhood more strongly doth enforce
The much-lamented lot of their divorce.
Themselves then of their losses guilty are
Who may, yet will not suffer a repair.
Those were Barbarian wives that did invent
Weeping to death at th' husband's monument,
But in more civil rites she doth approve
Her first, who ventures on a second love;
For else it may be thought if she refrain,
She sped so ill she durst not try again,
Up then my love, and choose some worthier one
Who may supply my room when I am gone;
So will the stock of our affection thrive
No less in death, than were I still alive.
And in my urn I shall rejoice, that I
Am both Testatour thus and legacy.

HENRY KING

To My Husband

When from the world, I shall be ta'en,
And from earth's necessary pain,
Then let no blacks be worn for me,
Not in a ring, my dear, by thee.
But this bright diamond, let it be
Worn in remembrance of me.
And when it sparkles in your eye,

Think 'tis my shadow passeth by.
For why, more bright you shall me see,
Than that or any gem can be.
Dress not the house with sable weed,
As if there was some dismal deed
Acted to be when I am gone,
There is no cause for me to mourn.
And let no badge of herald be
The sign of my antiquity.
It was my glory I did spring
From heaven's eternal powerful King:
To his bright palace heir am I.
It is his promise, he'll not lie.
By my dear brother lay me,
It was a promise made by thee,
And now I must bid thee adieu,
For I'm a-parting now from you.

'ELIZA'

Upon The Death Of Sir Albert Morton's Wife

He first deceased: she for a little tried
To live without him: liked it not, and died.

SIR HENRY WOTTON

Upon The Death Of Her Husband

(EXTRACT)

Yet, gentle shade! whether thou now does rove,
Thro' some blest vale, or ever verdant grove,
One moment listen to my grief and take
The softest vows that ever love can make.
For thee, all thoughts of pleasure I forgo,
For thee, my tears shall never cease to flow;
For thee at once I from the world retire,
To feed in silent shades a hopeless fire.

My bosom all thy image shall retain,
The full impression there shall still remain
As thou has taught my tender heart to prove
The noblest height and elegance of love,
That sacred passion I to thee confine.
My spotless faith shall be for ever thine.

ELIZABETH SINGER ROWE

Elegy On The Death Of Her Husband

(EXTRACT)

I envy air because it dare
Still breathe, and he not so;
Hate earth, that doth entomb his youth,
And who can blame my woe?

ANNE DACRE HOWARD

Epitaph To Sir William Dyer

My dearest dust, could not thy hasty day
Afford thy drowsy patience leave to stay
One hour longer: so that we might either
Sat up, or gone to bed together?
But since thy finished labour hath possessed
Thy weary limbs with early rest,
Enjoy it sweetly: and thy widow bride
Shall soon repose her by thy slumbering side.
Whose business, now, is only to prepare
My nightly dress, and call to prayer:
Mine eyes wax heavy and ye day grows old
The dew falls thick, my beloved grows cold.
Draw, draw ye closed curtains: and make room:
My dear, my dearest dust; I come, I come.

LADY CATHERINE DYER

The Anniversary

(EXTRACT)

. . . Only our love hath no decay;
This, no to-morrow hath, nor yesterday
Running it never runs from us away,
But truly keeps his first, last, everlasting day.
    Two graves must hide thine and my corse,
    If one might, death were no divorce.
Alas, as well as other Princes, we
(Who Prince enough in one another be,)
Must leave at last in death, these eyes, and ears,
Oft fed with true oaths, and with sweet salt tears;
    But souls where nothing dwells but love
(All other thoughts being inmates) then shall prove
This, or a love increasèd there above,
When bodies to their graves, souls from their graves remove.

JOHN DONNE

LOVE REMEMBERED

When You Are Old

When you are old and gray and full of sleep
   And nodding by the fire, take down this book,
   And slowly read, and dream of the soft look
Your eyes had once, and of their shadows deep;

How many loved your moments of glad grace,
   And loved your beauty with love false or true;
   But one man loved the pilgrim soul in you,
And loved the sorrows of your changing face.

And bending down beside the glowing bars
   Murmur, a little sadly, how love fled
   And paced upon the mountains overhead,
And hid his face amid a crowd of stars.

W.B. YEATS

Now Is Past

Now is past – the happy now
   When we together roved
Beneath the wildwood's oak-tree bough
   And nature said we loved.
     Winter's blast
The now since then has crept between,
   And left us both apart.
Winters that withered all the green
   Have froze the beating heart.
     Now is past.

Now is past since last we met
   Beneath the hazel bough;
Before the evening sun was set
   Her shadow stretched below.
     Autumn's blast
Has stained and blighted every bough;
   Wild strawberries like her lips
Have left the mosses green below,
   Her bloom's upon the hips.
     Now is the past.

Now is past, is changed again,
   The woods and fields are painted new.
Wild strawberries which both gathered then,
   None know now where they grew.
     The sky's o'ercast,
Wood strawberries faded from wood-rides,
   True love has no bed-fellow.
     Now is past.

JOHN CLARE

O That 'Twere Possible

O that 'twere possible
After long grief and pain
To find the arms of my true love
Round me once again! . . .

A shadow flits before me,
Not thou, but like to thee:
Ah, Christ! that it were possible
For one short hour to see
The souls we loved, that they might tell us
What and where they be!

ALFRED, LORD TENNYSON

Farewell To Juliet

I see you, Juliet, still, with your straw hat
Loaded with vines, and with your dear pale face,
On which those thirty years so lightly sat,
And the white outline of your muslin dress.
You wore a little fichu trimmed with lace
And crossed in front, as was the fashion then,
Bound at your waist with a broad band or sash,
All white and fresh and virginally plain.
There was a sound of shouting far away
Down in the valley, as they called to us,
And you, with hands clasped seeming still to pray
Patience of fate, stood listening to me thus
With heaving bosom. There a rose lay curled.
It was the reddest rose in all the world.

WILFRID BLUNT

The First Day

I wish I could remember the first day,
First hour, first moment of your meeting me,
If bright or dim the season, it might be
Summer or Winter for aught that I can say;
So unrecorded did it slip away,
So blind was I to see and to foresee,
So dull to mark the budding of my tree
That would not blossom yet for many a May,
If only I could recollect it, such
A day of days! I let it come and go
As traceless as a thaw of bygone snow;
It seemed to mean so little, meant so much;
If only now I could recall that touch,
First touch of hand in hand. – Did one but know!

CHRISTINA ROSSETTI

Early Love

Ah! I remember well (and how can I
But evermore remember well) when first
Our flame began, when scarce we knew what was
The flame we felt; when as we sat and sighed
And looked upon each other, and conceived
Not what we ailed – yet something we did ail;
And yet were well, and yet we were not well,
And what was our disease we could not tell.
Then would we kiss, then sigh, then look; and thus
In that first garden of our simpleness
We spent our childhood. But when years began
To reap the fruit of knowledge, ah, how then
Would she with graver looks, with sweet, stern brow,
Check my presumption and my forwardness;
    Yet still would give me flowers, still wound me, show
    What she would have me, yet not have me know.

SAMUEL DANIEL

The Chess-Board

    Irene, do you yet remember
Ere we were grown so sadly wise,
Those evenings in the bleak December,
Curtained warm from the snowy weather,
When you and I played chess together,
    Checkmated by each other's eyes?
    Ah, still I see your soft white hand
Hovering warm o'er queen and knight,
    Brave pawns in valiant battle stand:
The double castles guard the wings:
The bishop, bent on distant things,
Moves, sidling, through the fight,
    Our fingers touch; our glances meet,
    And falter; falls your golden hair

Against my cheek; your bosom sweet
Is heaving. Down the field, your queen
Rides slow her soldiery all between,
    And checks me unaware.

    Ah me! the little battle's done,
Dispersed is all its chivalry;
Full many a move, since then, have we
'Mid life's perplexing chequers made,
And many a game with fortune played, –
    What is it we have won?
    This, this at least – if this alone; –
That never, never, never more,
As in those old still nights of yore,
    (Ere we were grown so sadly wise)
    Can you and I shut out the skies,
Shut out the world, and wintry weather,
And, eyes exchanging warmth with eyes,
Play chess, as then we played, together!

EDWARD ROBERT BULWER LYTTON, FIRST EARL OF LYTTON

So, We'll Go No More A Roving

So, we'll go no more a roving
    So late into the night,
Though the heart be still as loving,
    And the moon be still as bright.

For the sword outwears its sheath,
    And the soul wears out the breast,
And the heart must pause to breathe,
    And love itself have rest.

Though the night was made for loving,
    And the day returns too soon,
Yet we'll go no more a roving
    By the light of the moon.

GEORGE GORDON, LORD BYRON

When Last We Parted

When last we parted, thou wert young and fair,
    How beautiful let fond remembrance say!
    Alas! since then old time has stolen away
Full thirty years, leaving my temples bare. —
So has it perished like a thing of air,
    The dream of love and youth! — now both are grey
    Yet still remembering that delightful day,
Though time with his cold touch has blanched my hair,
    Though I have suffered many years of pain
Since then, though I did never think to live
    To hear that voice or see those eyes again,
I can a sad but cordial greeting give,
And for thy welfare breathe as warm a prayer —
As when I loved thee young and fair.

                    CATHERINE MARIA FANSHAWE

Encounter

We meet again.
You are brief, staccato in your wonder as a leaf in autumn:
'It is a joy! . . . It has been so long!' . . .
As leaves — yellow, red, or brown — your words flutter down.
There is nothing to say, anyway.
You are you.
I can rub my hand against your coat —
It will be rough and my nails will catch upon the threads,
And your head will be held high, your lips will smile
For each passer-by.

You are no mystery to me:
I have grown wise with thinking on your beauty;
I could let your beauty slip like grains of sand
Between my fingers, and could find each grain again
And hold it in the hollow of my hand.

The sun lengthens our shadows into one;
We move along.
The sound of our feet against the stone pavement,
Swift and hard;
The sound of our feet descending a stair;
Warm air fawning about us,
Laughter that bursts like a red balloon, as soon forgotten.
Laughter, warm air, small painted chairs, a table, yellow cups, tea —
My thoughts lie like dust upon the bloom of the room.

We are together;
There is still singing truth of our youth;
We may go as a feather goes beyond the wind that blows it.

'The days have been so very long away from you' —
You light a cigarette —
'So very long!' The smoke curls a ring around your suffering.

Ah well, your lies are as a warmth of sun pressing the lids over
     my eyes,
And I am tired.
I would remember summer: hours that fell as fruit upon the ground,
As fruit were held, tasted, thrown away;
Each day opening its petals to another day.
Summer! Tendrils of heat drawing us down —
Sweet, sweet earth!
Rain lisping to flowers . . .

'Do you still take three lumps in your tea?' — you smile,
Lean forward as you speak; shadows shift:
Your hair is smooth as lacquer, light glides upon it —
'And still get perfume from Piver?'
I feel the color in my cheek.

What does it matter anyway?
The breath of winter blurs the window-pane —
And if we love again, what does it matter?
I would remember summer:
There is still the harvest moon — soon it will be over,
Very soon.

You rise, you are sorry, you must go —
'It was a joy! . . . It has been so long!'
We reach the street.

And I am swayed as a blade of grass beneath the wind.
As the wind you are gone.

MARION STROBEL

A May Song

A little while my love and I
    Before the mowing of the hay,
Twined daisy-chains and cowslip balls,
And carolled glees and madrigals,
    Before the hay, beneath the may,
My love (who loved me then) and I.

For long years now my love and I
    Tread severed paths to varied ends;
We sometimes meet, and sometimes say
The trivial things of every day,
    And meet as comrades, meet as friends,
My love (who loved me once) and I.

But never more my love and I
    Will wander forth, as once, together,
Or sing the songs we used to sing
    In spring-time, in the cloudless weather:
Some chord is mute that used to ring,
    Some word forgot we used to say
    Amongst the may, before the hay,
My love (who loves me not) and I.

MARY MONTGOMERIE, LADY CURRIE

Recollection Of First Love

When I recall your form and face
More than you I recall
To come into a meeting-place
Where no leaves fall:
The years walk round this secret garth
But cannot change its guarded earth.

I have known women fonder far
Than you; more fair, more kind:
Women whose passionate faces are
Flowers in the mind:
But as a tall tree, stem on stem,
Your presence overshadows them.

They quicken from my sentient day
And stir my body's need;
But you had fixèd roots ere they
Down-dropped in seed:
They can but copy all I found
When you alone grew in this ground.

You are reborn from changeless loam
And are a changeless shade:
Your feet had paced the paths to Rome
Ere Rome was made:
Under your eyes great towers down fell
Before that Trojan citadel.

Time, who is knocking at the gate,
Cannot make you all his boast:
Our garden shall be desolate
But you – a ghost
Timeless; as beauty's timeless norm
You are in passion and in form.

WILLIAM SOUTAR

A Second Attempt

Thirty years after
I began again
An old-time passion:
And it seemed as fresh as when
The first day ventured on:
When mutely I would waft her
In love's past fashion
Dreams much dwelt upon,
Dreams I wished she knew.

I went the course through,
From love's fresh-found sensation –
Remembered still so well –
To worn words charged anew,
That left no more to tell:
Thence to hot hopes and fears,
And thence to consummation,
And thence to sober years,
Markless, and mellow-hued.

Firm the whole fabric stood,
Or seemed to stand, and sound
As it had stood before.
But nothing backward climbs,
And when I looked around
As at the former times,
There was life – pale and hoar;
And slow it said to me,
'Twice-over cannot be!'

THOMAS HARDY

Once Fondly Loved

Once fondly loved, and still remembered dear,
　　Sweet early object of my youthful vows,
Accept this mark of friendship, warm, sincere –
　　Friendship! 'tis all cold duty now allows: –

And when you read the simple, artless rhymes,
　　One friendly sigh for him – he asks no more –
Who distant burns in flaming torrid climes,
　　Or haply lies beneath th' Atlantic roar.

ROBERT BURNS

Non Sum Qualis Eram Bonæ Sub Regno Cynaræ

Last night, ah, yesternight, betwixt her lips and mine
There fell thy shadow, Cynara! thy breath was shed
Upon my soul between the kisses and the wine;
And I was desolate and sick of an old passion,
　　Yea, I was desolate and bowed my head:
I have been faithful to thee, Cynara! in my fashion.

All night upon mine heart I felt her warm heart beat,
Night-long within mine arms in love and sleep she lay;
Surely the kisses of her bought red mouth were sweet;
But I was desolate and sick of an old passion,
　　When I awoke and found the dawn was gray:
I have been faithful to thee, Cynara! in my fashion.

I have forgot much, Cynara! gone with the wind,
Flung roses, roses riotously with the throng,
Dancing, to put thy pale lost lilies out of mind;
But I was desolate and sick of an old passion,
　　Yea, all the time, because the dance was long:
I have been faithful to thee, Cynara! in my fashion.

I cried for madder music and for stronger wine,
But when the feast is finished and the lamps expire,
Then falls thy shadow, Cynara! the night is thine;
And I am desolate and sick of an old passion,
    Yea, hungry for the lips of my desire:
I have been faithful to thee, Cynara! in my fashion.

ERNEST DOWSON

Song

I made another garden, yea,
    For my new love;
I left the dead rose where it lay,
    And set the new above.
Why did the summer not begin?
    Why did my heart not haste?
My old love came and walked therein,
    And laid the garden waste.

She entered with her weary smile,
    Just as of old;
She looked around a little while,
    And shivered at the cold.
Her passing touch was death to all,
    Her passing look a blight:
She made the white rose-petals fall,
    And turned the red rose white.

Her pale robe, clinging to the grass,
    Seemed like a snake
That bit the grass and ground, alas!
    And a sad trail did make.
She went up slowly to the gate;
    And there, just as of yore,
She turned back at the last to wait,
    And say farewell once more.

ARTHUR O'SHAUGHNESSY

The Flight

Look back with longing eyes and know that I will follow,
Lift me up in your love as a light wing lifts a swallow,
Let our flight be far in sun or blowing rain –
But what if I heard my first love calling me again?

Hold me on your heart as the brave sea holds the foam,
Take me far away to the hills that hide your home:
Peace shall thatch the roof and love shall latch the door –
But what if I heard my first love calling me again?

SARA TEASDALE

Echo

Come to me in the silence of the night;
    Come in the speaking silence of a dream;
Come with soft rounded cheeks and eyes as bright
    As sunlight on a stream;
        Come back in tears,
O memory, hope, love of finished years.

Oh dream how sweet, too sweet, too bitter sweet,
    Whose wakening should have been in paradise,
Where souls brimful of love abide and meet;
    Where thirsting longing eyes
        Watch the slow door
That opening, letting in, lets out no more.

Yet come to me in dreams, that I may live
    My very life again tho' cold in death:
Come back to me in dreams, that I may give
    Pulse for pulse, breath for breath:
        Speak low, lean low,
As long ago, my love, how long ago.

CHRISTINA ROSSETTI

If I Forget

If I forget
The salt creek may forget the ocean;
   If I forget
The heart whence flowed my heart's bright motion,
May I sink meanlier than the worst,
Abandoned, outcast, crushed, accurst, –
   If I forget.

   Though you forget,
No word of mine shall mar your pleasure;
   Though you forget, –
You filled my barren life with treasure;
You may withdraw the gift you gave,
You still are queen, I still am slave,
   Though you forget.

THOMAS HARDY

Vain Resolves

I said: 'There is an end of my desire:
Now have I sown, and I have harvested,
And these are ashes of an ancient fire,
Which, verily, shall not be quickened.
Now will I take me to a place of peace,
Forget mine heart's desire;
In solitude and prayer, work out my soul's release.

'I shall forget her eyes, how cold they were;
Forget her voice, how soft it was and low,
With all my singing that she did not hear,
And all my service that she did not know.
I shall not hold the merest memory
Of any days that were,
Within those solitudes where I will fasten me.'

And once she passed, and once she raised her eyes,
And smiled for courtesy, and nothing said:
And suddenly the old flame did uprise,
And all my dead desire was quickened.
Yea! as it hath been, it shall ever be,
Most passionless, pure eyes!
Which never shall grow soft, nor change, nor pity me.

ERNEST DOWSON

The Lover Mourns
For The Loss Of Love

Pale brows, still hands and dim hair,
· I had a beautiful friend
And dreamed that the old despair
Would end in love in the end:
She looked in my heart one day
And saw your image was there;
She has gone weeping away.

W.B. YEATS

The Cold Change

In the cold change which time hath wrought on love
    (The snowy winter of his summer prime),
Should a chance sigh or sudden tear-drop move
    Thy heart to memory of the olden time;
Turn not to gaze on me with pitying eyes,
    Nor mock me with a withered hope renewed;
But from the bower we both have loved, arise
    And leave me to my barren solitude!

What boots it that a momentary flame
    Shoots from the ashes of a dying fire?
We gaze upon the hearth from whence it came,
    And know the exhausted embers must expire:
Therefore no pity, or my heart will break;
Be cold, be careless – for thy past love's sake!

CAROLINE NORTON

Lost Love

Who wins his love shall lose her,
    Who lose her shall gain,
For still the spirit woos her,
    A soul without a stain;
And memory still pursues her
    With longings not in vain!

He loses her who gains her,
    Who watches day by day
The dust of time that stains her,
    The griefs that leave her gray –
The flesh that yet enchains her
    Whose grace hath passed away!

Oh, happier he who gains not
    The love some seem to gain:
The joy that custom stains not
    Shall still with him remain;
The loveliness that wanes not,
    The love that ne'er can wane.

In dreams she grows not older
    The lands of dream among;
Though all the world wax colder,
    Though all the songs be sung,
In dreams doth he behold her
    Still fair and kind and young.

ANDREW LANG

Lavender

The gently quiet murmur of the summer rain,
Falling on attic roofs,
Brings to the store of old rejected things, below
In the gabled darkened room,
The thought of youth;
As soft love-touches
On the arched and narrowed shoulders of a spinster
May recall
The failing hopes and unremembered joys.
And so on my heart,
Filled with the past's old dusty things,
Falls now the sweet and gentle softness of your voice.

CONSTANCE ENSLOW

Music

Music, when soft voices die,
Vibrates in the memory –
Odours, when sweet violets sicken,
Live within the sense they quicken.
Rose leaves, when the rose is dead,
Are heaped for the belovèd's bed;
And so thy thoughts, when thou art gone,
Love itself shall slumber on.

PERCY BYSSHE SHELLEY

Those Who Love

Those who love the most,
Do not talk of their love,
Francesca, Guinevere,
Deirdre, Iseult, Heloise,
In the fragrant gardens of heaven
Are silent, or speak if at all
Of fragile inconsequent things.

And a woman I used to know
Who loved one man from her youth,
Against the strength of the fates
Fighting in somber pride
Never spoke of this thing.
But hearing his name by chance,
A light would pass over her face.

SARA TEASDALE

INDEX OF POETS & TITLES

INDEX OF FIRST LINES